# Don't Jump to Conclusions
# Without a Bungee Cord

# Don't Jump to Conclusions Without a Bungee Cord

## AND OTHER WISE ADVICE

Devotions for Teens From the Book of Proverbs

## Martha Bolton

SERVANT PUBLICATIONS
ANN ARBOR, MICHIGAN

Vine Books is an imprint of Servant Publications especially designed to
serve evangelical Christians.

Published by Servant Publications
P.O. Box 8617
Ann Arbor, Michigan 48107

Cover design: PAZ Design Group
Cover illustration: Pat Binder

    00  01  02  10  9  8  7  6  5  4  3

Printed in the United States of America
ISBN 1-56955-080-8


LIBRARY OF CONGRESS CATALOGING-IN-PUBLICATION DATA

Bolton, Martha, 1951-
Don't jump to conclusions without a bungee cord / Martha Bolton.
    p.    cm.
Summary: Ninety devotional readings based on the Book of Proverbs,
helping readers understand how their choices reflect God's priorities and
including Scripture passages, short prayers, and "bumper sticker"
thoughts to ponder.
ISBN (invalid) 1-56955-080-0 (alk. paper)
1. Youth Prayer-books and devotions—English.    2. Bible. O.T. Proverbs
Meditations—Juvenile literature.    [1. Prayer books and devotions.    2.
Bible. O.T. Proverbs Meditations.]    I. Title.
BV4850.B6    1999
242'.63—dc21                                          99-30481
                                                       CIP

## Dedication

To my nephew, Joe—
may the force (of laughter and God's love)
always be with you.

# Contents

# Acknowledgments

Thank you to:

My husband, Russ, who has always been willing to go anywhere in life with me ... except bungee jumping.

My sons, Russ, Matt, and Tony, who grew up thinking all food is supposed to be black.

To my daughter-in-law, Nicole, and granddaughter, Kiana, for giving me someone to do "girl" things with.

And to my editor, Heidi Hess, whose sweet,
gentle spirit made me hardly notice the whip.
(Ah, deadlines ... how quickly they sneak up on us!)

# ONE

# Wise Up!

According to King Solomon, wisdom is a quality we should pursue with all our strength. Those who possess wisdom save themselves a lot of trouble.

Wisdom is what keeps us from saying to a sumo-wrestler, "You gonna make me?"

Wisdom is why we don't climb trees to get a better look at lightning.

Wisdom is what stops us from ordering anything in the school cafeteria with the word "Surprise" in the name.

Wisdom is why we don't ride that double backward loop roller coaster after eating two chili dogs and a sausage pizza.... Or sit in front of someone who did.

Wisdom is what keeps us from cleaning out our closet without a hard hat and a search-and-rescue team on standby.

And wisdom is the reason none of my dinner guests ever ask for seconds.

Wisdom—don't leave home without it.

## THOUGHTS TO PONDER

Think of a time you did something *wise*. What happened?

Think of a time you did something *unwise*. What happened?

Why do you think wisdom is something we should pray for?

## BUMPER STICKER OF THE DAY

When it comes to making decisions, it's OK to be a wiseguy.

## SCRIPTURE TO STAND ON

Wisdom is supreme; therefore get wisdom.
Though it cost all you have, get understanding.

PROVERBS 4:7

## HELLO AGAIN, LORD...

Lord, grant me wisdom in all my decisions, and a LOT of wisdom before I take my SATs.

# TWO

# First Class, Wrong Flight

A few years ago Mark Lowry, Tony Wood, and I wrote a song called "First Class, Wrong Flight." It's about a man who is given a first-class ticket, but it's for the wrong flight.

Sure, he's traveling in style. He's in the company of CEOs, VIPs, and movie stars. His dinner is being served on real china instead of in a cardboard box. He's got all the good magazines, a recliner seat, and unlimited beverages (served in crystal instead of plastic cups). His every desire is being met. There's only one problem. He's not going where he wants to go.

Unfortunately, some of us are traveling through life that way. We're doing it in style, making sure our every desire is being met. We rub shoulders with the elite, the "in" crowd, as we fly from place to place. But we're traveling in the wrong direction—going where the world wants us to go, instead of following the path God has for us. What's the point of all the luxury, of lookin' good, if, when we reach the end of our journey, we're nowhere near the place God wanted us to be?

## THOUGHTS TO PONDER

Do you feel you're headed in the direction God wants you to go?

Why is arriving at our intended destination more important than the comforts (or discomforts) of the journey?

## BUMPER STICKER FOR THE DAY

> **Seeking adventure?
> Journey to the Center of His Will.**

## SCRIPTURE TO STAND ON

In his heart a man plans his course,
but the Lord determines his steps.

PROVERBS 16:9

## HELLO AGAIN, LORD...

Lord, before I get too comfortable, remind me to check my ticket.

# THREE

# Testing Ground

If you've got an exam coming up, you may be wishing there was no such thing as testing. It's a lot of work staying up all night studying, reading chapter after chapter, and memorizing all your study notes. On the other hand, you'll never know for sure how much you really know about that subject until someone tests you on it.

Do you realize the same is true of our faith? We can say we love the Lord, we can say we want to serve him, we can say we totally trust him, but until there's a test, we'll never really know for sure the depths of our faith.

Maybe that's why God allows us to go through tests from time to time. When we have to lean on that faith we've been talking about, when we have to trust the God we've been introducing to others, when we have to come face to face with our beliefs and match up our walk with our talk, something happens to us. Either we pass the test and understand our faith even more, or we realize we don't have the faith we thought we had and have to go back and hit the books again. Or in this case, the Book, God's Word.

Tests are never fun. Pop quizzes don't provide a lot of laughs either. But if we've been studying God's Word, if we've been learning his ways, if we've prepared ourselves, then we don't have to fear the test. We only have to grow from it.

## THOUGHTS TO PONDER

Have you had a "test of faith" lately?

Do you think it made you stronger or weaker in your faith? Why?

## BUMPER STICKER FOR THE DAY

God allows our faith to be tested,
not so he'll know how strong it is,
but so we will.

## SCRIPTURE TO STAND ON

The crucible for silver and the furnace
for gold, but the Lord tests the heart.

PROVERBS 17:3

## HELLO AGAIN, LORD...

Lord, thank you for the tests that solidify my faith in you.

# FOUR

# Pumpkin Pies and Prayer

My youngest son Tony's favorite dessert is pumpkin pie. It's a difficult dessert to make, but well worth the effort. The main problem with pumpkin pie is in the timing. If you take it out of the oven too soon, you end up with pumpkin soup. If you leave it in too long, you end up with pumpkin jerkey. Pumpkin pie has to be cooked just right.

Still, we get tired of waiting, so we keep opening the oven door, checking on its progress. Unfortunately, this doesn't help. Our impatience is actually keeping the pie from getting done.

Praying can be a little like baking a pie. Again, timing is everything. God answers our prayers at just the right time. It may not be our right time, but it's always his. It can be hard to wait—our human nature isn't very patient. We want our requests granted now, not later; today, not tomorrow.

Some people try to make deals with God, trying to hurry him along. But God knows if he answers our prayers when we want them answered, we might end up with pumpkin soup. He also knows that making us wait too long could bring discouragement, and that isn't good either.

So, when it comes to prayers and pumpkin pies, all we can do is depend upon the right timing. For the pie, we have to trust the recipe. For our prayers, we have to trust that God has promised to meet each and every one of his children's needs in his perfect time.

## THOUGHTS TO PONDER

Have you ever requested something from God and you grew tired of waiting for the answer?

Why do you think you haven't received your answer yet? What are you learning from the experience?

## BUMPER STICKER FOR THE DAY

Did you hear about the trapeze artist who didn't think timing was important? Everyone soon saw he was flat wrong.

## SCRIPTURE TO STAND ON

The Lord is far from the wicked
but he hears the prayer of the righteous.

PROVERBS 15:29

## HELLO AGAIN, LORD...

Lord, when I pray for my needs, help me to realize that patience might be one of them.

# FIVE

# In My Humble Opinion

**H**ave you ever met one of those overachievers, whose first words to you sounded like a fourteen-page resumé? They've won beauty contests and spelling bees, MVP awards and Ivy League scholarships ... even a perfect attendance award in kindergarten. They could go on and on, but it's easier to just hand you their business card and let you talk to their Achievements Manager.

It's easy to start feeling inadequate in the company of someone like this, especially when you were just about to tell them of your promotion to Fries Manager at a local fast food restaurant. But don't. Never allow someone else's over-inflated ego to deflate yours.

God's opinion of you is the only one that really counts, and he measures how important you are very differently than others do. He doesn't care who's the prettiest, the smartest, or the most popular. It's not important to him if we're the most talented athlete to ever step onto the playing field. God doesn't care about how many achievements we can list on our resumés. What God cares about is what holds the highest place in our heart—those achievements, or loving him.

## THOUGHTS TO PONDER

What do you think makes some people feel they have to brag?

Why do you think God is interested in where we've placed our achievements in our hearts?

## BUMPER STICKER FOR THE DAY

> **The best resumé is
> how you live your life.**

## SCRIPTURE TO STAND ON

Let another praise you, and not your own mouth;
someone else, and not your own lips.

PROVERBS 27:2

## HELLO AGAIN, LORD...

Lord, I'm nothing without you. Forgive me when I try to be.

# SIX

# Alive and Well

I used to write a lot of poetry when I was a teenager. I would tape the poems on the wall above my bed (it was cheaper than wallpaper). I had about thirty-five poems—some long, some short, some funny, some serious. I was about fourteen when I wrote this one:

> I was walking through a valley once
> where God did not exist.
> I had weighed both all the pros and cons
> and thus concluded this:
> The story of the God creator
> was a fairy tale of old.
> That he's alive and well today?
> The greatest fiction ever sold!
> I walked on throughout my valley,
> proudly held my head up high;
> until one day I heard a voice
> as thunder from the sky.
> It called my name. I froze with fear!
> My hair stood on my head!
> And then I heard that voice proclaim,
> "Just who'd you say was dead?"

Skeptics don't understand God's existence, so they deny it. But God exists in spite of our unbelief, he gives in spite of our selfishness, and he loves in spite of our unworthiness.

Dead? Hardly. Alive and well and awesome? You'd better believe it!

## THOUGHTS TO PONDER

Have you ever doubted God's existence? What made you conclude that he exists and cares about you?

Why do you think some people refuse to see God's existence?

## BUMPER STICKER FOR THE DAY

> **People who believe God is dead usually resurrect him whenever they're in trouble.**

## SCRIPTURE TO STAND ON

Who has gathered up the wind in the hollow of his hands?
Who has wrapped up the waters in his cloak?
Who has established all the ends of the earth?

PROVERBS 30:4

## HELLO AGAIN, LORD...

Lord, thank you for being real, for being alive, and for loving me as you do.

# SEVEN

# Giving It All

On December 8, 1988, around four o'clock in the morning, two Los Angeles Police patrol cars, both responding to an emergency call, collided head-on at the intersection of Fifth and Wall Street in downtown Los Angeles. My husband, Sergeant Russ Bolton, was the watch commander that evening and received the initial news of the fatal accident.

Three officers were killed. The force of the impact was so great, it ripped the badge off the shirt of one of the officers and sent it flying some one hundred feet away. One young recruit, the only officer wearing a seatbelt, was the sole survivor.

This particular intersection is in the heart of downtown. On just about every corner you can find displaced men, women, and children walking the streets at all hours of the day and night in search of shelter, food, and a little bit of hope. These are people who don't know where their next meal is coming from, people who seemingly have plenty of their own problems to worry about.

The morning following the accident, however, an elderly woman walked into the lobby of the Central Division police station. Dressed in worn-out, secondhand clothing, she approached the officer at the front desk and handed him a card along with a single artificial flower standing tall and proud in a small plastic vase. The lady explained that the card had been signed by several dozen of the homeless of that area, and both the card and the flower had been purchased with a collection she had taken up among the street people. It was a simple gift, but it caught the eye and the heart of everyone around.

Out of all the flowers, cards, and expressions of grief that flooded the precinct that day, no one will ever forget the one given by a group of people who temporarily forgot their own needs and gave all they had to encourage someone else.

Too often we don't think we can do enough to lift someone's burden, so we don't do anything. But that lady didn't look at what she couldn't do. She looked at what she could do, and she did it.

## THOUGHTS TO PONDER

Is there someone to whom you've been waiting to show your love and concern, but you didn't think you could do enough?

What small thing can you do to show your love right now?

## BUMPER STICKER FOR THE DAY

> **Don't wait to help lift someone's weight.**

## SCRIPTURE TO STAND ON

Rich and poor have this in common:
The Lord is the Maker of them all.

PROVERBS 22:2

## HELLO AGAIN, LORD...

Lord, instead of being bound by my limitations, may I be driven by my heart.

# EIGHT

# Take Two Laughs and Call Me in the Morning

George Burns lived to be a hundred. Bob Hope's going strong well into his nineties. Lucille Ball, Danny Thomas, Minnie Pearl, and Gracie Allen all lived long lives, too, while Phyllis Diller, Milton Berle, Steve Allen, and Johnny Carson are all still around and enjoying life to the fullest.

These comedians discovered an important key to living a long and happy life. Laughter. Laughter has even been proven to help you lose weight. It's been reported that a hearty laugh will burn off thirty-five calories. So which sounds like more fun to you: 150 push-ups or watching an "I Love Lucy" rerun?

The most important thing to remember about laughter is that it's God-ordained. If our heavenly Father didn't believe in a good clean joke, why did he create us with the ability to respond to it? He's the one who gave us the equipment to laugh. No doubt he intended for us to use it. And use it often. I've never once heard of someone dying from an overactive sense of humor.

Not that laughter is 100 percent safe. I wouldn't recommend it during a high dive. If you don't close your mouth in time, you could drown. And if you laugh while drinking a glass of milk, you can suck the liquid up your nose and choke to death. But for the most part, laughter is one of the healthiest things you can do for your body.

So, lighten up! Laughter is good medicine! Take a healthy dose every day!

## THOUGHTS TO PONDER

On most days do you see lots of things to laugh about, or do you tend to dwell on the negative too much?

What's the funniest thing that's ever happened to you in your life?

## BUMPER STICKER FOR THE DAY

Laughter—the most effective antidepressant around.

## SCRIPTURE TO STAND ON

A cheerful heart is good medicine.

PROVERBS 17:22

## HELLO AGAIN, LORD...

Lord, may I never forget the importance of laughter in my life. By the way, did you hear the one about ... oh, never mind, you're omniscient. You already know the punchline.

# NINE
# Shhh!

The other day a friend told me something in confidence—something, she said, I'd have to take to my grave. I jokingly remarked that I've been told so many things that I have to take to my grave, they're going to have to bury me in two plots!

When someone confides in you, they're giving you a great responsibility. They're trusting you with their problem, their reputation, their pain, their future. That's not something to be taken lightly. Friends who break a confidence risk a lot, not the least of which is their friendship.

Naturally, if your friend tells you about something in confidence that you can't in good conscience keep to yourself—if that person's life may be in danger or some other serious matter which needs professional intervention—then you must encourage that person to talk to their pastor, parents, school counselor, police, or someone else who can give them proper guidance.

But if your friend's situation isn't the kind that requires intervention, if they're just wanting to talk with you about a situation that, for whatever reason, they don't feel they can share with anyone else, then honor that confidence. Don't be the type of person who can't be trusted with personal matters. Lock their story away until they themselves are ready to share it with others. Sharing it is their job, not yours. Your job is just to listen.

## THOUGHTS TO PONDER

Has anyone ever broken one of your confidences? How did that make you feel?

Why do you think it's important to be the kind of person your friends can trust?

## BUMPER STICKER FOR THE DAY

> When it comes to keeping a secret,
> be a safe, not a sieve.

## SCRIPTURE TO STAND ON

A gossip betrays a confidence;
so avoid a man who talks too much.

PROVERBS 20:19

## HELLO AGAIN, LORD...

Lord, help me to be the kind of confidant I want my friends to be to me.

# TEN

# Identity Crisis

**D**o you ever wish you were someone else? Are your dreams documentaries of other people's lives? Do you feel like everyone's smarter, more talented, and better looking than you?

Most of us, if we're honest with ourselves, suffer or have suffered from feelings of inadequacy. Maybe someone in our life makes us feel that way, or some past emotional hurt. No matter where it's coming from, though, the simple fact is we *are* significant. Especially to Jesus. Learning to love and appreciate who we are—the gift of our personalities—is an important part of life.

Throughout the Scriptures, Jesus went out of his way to make the most insignificant people feel significant. From the woman at the well, to the woman caught in adultery, to Zaccheus the tax collector, Jesus cared equally as much for those whom the world rejected as he did for anyone else.

When we come to Jesus, he doesn't ask for three personal references and our last two paycheck stubs. We don't need a background check or a security clearance. He loves us not for what we bring to him but for who we *are*. There's no place for feelings of inadequacy in the shadow of his cross.

## THOUGHTS TO PONDER

If you were the only person in the world, do you think Jesus would have still died for you?

Since Jesus gave his life for you, how much does that mean you're worth?

## BUMPER STICKER FOR THE DAY

> If any of us were worthy of Christ's love, he never would have had to die.

## SCRIPTURE TO STAND ON

A gift is as a precious stone in the eyes of him that hath it.

PROVERBS 17:8, KJV

## HELLO AGAIN, LORD...

Lord, may I always see my value through your eyes.

# ELEVEN
## Tickets, Please

One woman I know won't go to church because of the lack of love shown to her by a couple of professing Christians in her life. Another acquaintance turned his back on God years ago because of the judgmental attitudes of some of the members of his church.

It's hurtful to be around those who profess Christianity, but do not live it out. But how we react to people like that can be just as wrong.

Say you're going on a train trip. You've got your ticket in your hand and you're ready to board. While you're standing in line, though, you happen to notice a group of people trying to board with some tickets they made up themselves. If you can tell the difference from twenty feet away, you're sure others will notice it, too. But nobody does.

The people with the fake tickets are allowed to go ahead and walk up the boarding ramp just like everyone else. As they stand there flaunting their self-made tickets, you say to yourself, "Hey, if they're being allowed on board, what good is my ticket?" So you rip yours up and throw it away.

The train begins pulling out of the station, and you can't help but feel bitter about the unfairness of the whole thing. After all, you got your ticket the right way. It's the official ticket. You've held on to it all these years, never once losing sight of it. But now it appears you did it all in vain.

The train chugs along the track. As it passes you, you glance inside one of the windows and see the unauthorized passengers partying and laughing and bragging about how they faked their way on board. "I can't believe they're getting away with this," you think to yourself.

But just then, the train stops, and out roll the unticketed passengers. Finally, you say to yourself, someone noticed the phony tickets and kicked the impostors off the train. As the train resumes its journey up the hill, you feel satisfied. Justice was served. At long last the fakers were unmasked and kicked off the train. They're not going anywhere.

Then again, neither are you.

## THOUGHTS TO PONDER

Have you been letting other people's behavior take your eyes off Jesus?

Why is it important to focus on our own journey?

## BUMPER STICKER FOR THE DAY

> Jesus didn't say, "Follow everyone."
> He said, "Follow Me."

## SCRIPTURE TO STAND ON

Does not he who weighs the heart perceive it?
Does not he who guards your life know it?
Will he not repay each person according to what he has done?

PROVERBS 24:12

## HELLO AGAIN, LORD...

Lord, help me not to blame you for the shortcomings of others.

## TWELVE

# Been There—Survived That

An artist gains perspective by extending his arm and comparing the subject of his artwork to the size of his thumb. A writer lets her manuscript sit for several weeks to gain a better perspective before she resumes working on it. A chef will ask someone to give him a second opinion on one of his culinary masterpieces, to make sure his liver and dumplings are as delectable as he thinks they are.

It's important to have perspective.

Once while traveling from Nashville to Los Angeles, my assigned seat on the airplane was next to a woman who had been a pilot during World War II. Throughout the flight she shared her fascinating war stories with me. I was grateful for this, because it took my mind off the pilot's announcement—Los Angeles was having thunderstorms that we'd be flying through to make our landing. (Frankly, I don't know why pilots make announcements like that. Don't they realize some of us enjoy living in denial?)

When it came time for us to land, we discovered the pilot had been right. Los Angeles was in the middle of a storm. We descended as far as we could, then pulled back up to make our approach from another angle. Even then, the cloud cover was so thick we couldn't see land until we were almost on top of it. When it touched down, the plane was still going so fast that my purse slid almost to the cockpit.

Finally, after what seemed like an eternity, the aircraft came to a screeching stop. The lady looked at me, smiled, and calmly said, "Well, that was a nice landing."

Glancing back at her through my hair, which was now in my face, I could see she was serious. Perspective. She must have made some pretty harrowing landings during the war. From her perspective, this landing was a good one. From my perspective, I expected to meet St. Peter at the gate when we deplaned.

Some of the hard times in life come our way primarily to give us perspective. Today's crisis doesn't look so bad when we recall how God brought us through yesterday's. Having perspective can also help us encourage others who are whiteknuckling their way from one turbulent storm of life to another. Because of what we've been through, we can say with confidence, "Just hang on a little longer. Things'll get better. God's in control. Relax."

## THOUGHTS TO PONDER

What are some perspectives that you've gained throughout your life?

Who might you be able to help by sharing them?

## BUMPER STICKER FOR THE DAY

> **Without perspective,
> there would be no masterpieces.**

## SCRIPTURE TO STAND ON

The corrections of discipline are the way to life.

PROVERBS 6:23

## HELLO AGAIN, LORD...

May my experiences teach me to experience your peace.

# THIRTEEN

# That's What Mirrors Are For

Ever wonder why Jesus dined with publicans and sinners, but never seemed to have a good word to say about the Pharisees? After all, the Pharisees were the "church crowd" of his day. You'd think they had a lot in common.

We find a clue in the story of the woman caught in adultery (see Jn 8:1-11). Jesus was sending us a message when he wrote the dirty sins of her accusers in the dirt. He was warning us against the sin of self-righteousness.

Years ago a well-known figure in the Christian community confessed to having committed adultery. While he was clearly in the wrong, and said so in his plea for forgiveness, there were those within the church who simply could not forgive him.

People who were guilty of pride condemned him.

People who were guilty of jealousy condemned him.

People who were guilty of greed and gluttony condemned him.

People who were guilty of gossip and backbiting condemned him, too.

We must never excuse sin—the Bible clearly warns us that adultery is wrong. But it also warns us against all sin—even the less obvious ones we tend to overlook in ourselves.

Before we start throwing stones at a brother or sister, maybe we should stop and consider what Jesus could write on the ground about us. If we did, we might just drop the stones and walk away before the writing starts.

## THOUGHTS TO PONDER

Think about some of the people you need to forgive.

Think about some things you've been forgiven for, or need forgiveness for.

## BUMPER STICKER FOR THE DAY

> A fellow believer's moral failure
> should drive us to our knees,
> not to our phones.

## SCRIPTURE TO STAND ON

Who can say, "I have kept my heart pure;
I am clean and without sin"?

PROVERBS 20:9

## HELLO AGAIN, LORD...

Lord, help me to see the sins of others through the same grace that you see mine.

# FOURTEEN

# A Humbling Experience

Each year the Christian Booksellers Association holds a convention in a different city across the nation. It's an opportunity for bookstore owners to see what's new on the market, place their orders for the coming year, and get books, CDs, and other products autographed by authors and recording artists.

I'll never forget the very first one I was invited to attend. My autograph session was held simultaneously with one for Carman, Jerry Falwell, and Kenneth Taylor. I'm not saying how many people came to my booth, but I was signing my autographs in calligraphy!

And just recently I was telling a good friend that I'd been nominated for a Dove Award. I guess she didn't quite catch what I had said. "So, what do they give the Dumb Award for?" she asked, ever so sincerely.

It's not just me. On one of the Bob Hope USO tours, a fellow writer was asked to pose for a picture with a soldier. Flattered, he agreed. He struck a pose for the camera, but before the soldier snapped the picture, he told him to turn around. The soldier really wanted a picture of the caricature of Bob Hope on the back of the writer's jacket.

Life can be humbling. Just when you think you're on top of the world, the world turns and someone else is up there. Then it turns again, and it's another person's turn. Fame is fleeting. People who are on the cover of *Newsweek* and *People* magazine today will be a footnote in those magazines tomorrow.

A humble spirit takes it all in stride. So, if you ever start to think more of yourself than you ought to, read what it says in Isaiah 51:1, "Look to the rock from which you were cut and to the quarry from which you were hewn."

## THOUGHTS TO PONDER

Have you ever had a humbling experience? Write it down.

Why do you think God brings honor to the humble?

## BUMPER STICKER FOR THE DAY

> Someone who's proud of their humility
> probably doesn't really have it.

## SCRIPTURE TO STAND ON

Humility comes before honor.

PROVERBS 15:33

## HELLO AGAIN, LORD ...

Lord, help me to remember that putting myself last is the quickest way to the front of the line.

# FIFTEEN

# What'd You Say?

A doctor once told me about an elderly lady entrusted into her care. The lady was going to have to be sent to Oakdale Convalescent Home. However, the doctor, who was new to town, mistakenly thought the name of the convalescent home was Oak Grove. Oak Grove happened to be the name of the town's cemetery. When the doctor broke the news to the lady, the conversation went something like this:

"I'm going to be sending you to Oak Grove," the doctor said, glancing over her chart.

The woman's eyes widened. "But I don't want to go to Oak Grove!" she said.

"Sorry, sweetie," the doctor continued. "But you have to go to Oak Grove."

"Why do I have to go to Oak Grove?"

"They're waiting for you," she said. "Besides, you'll like it there. It's peaceful and quiet and...."

"But I'm not ready to go to Oak Grove!" the lady pleaded.

"Sure, you are, honey," the doctor said. "And I'm going to be sending you there in a day and a half!"

Luckily, the doctor eventually realized her mistake and sent the woman to the right place! Years later, she can laugh about it. All's well that ends well. But it's a good illustration of how important our words are. Every last one of them.

## THOUGHTS TO PONDER

Have you ever been involved in a misunderstanding? What happened?

In your opinion, what's the best way to handle a misunderstanding?

## BUMPER STICKER FOR THE DAY

> Some misunderstandings
> can have grave consequences.

## SCRIPTURE TO STAND ON

A man finds joy in giving an apt reply—
how good is a timely word!

PROVERBS 15:23

## HELLO AGAIN, LORD...

Lord, help me to edit the words I speak before they exit my mouth.

# SIXTEEN
## The Best Laid Plans

Two decades ago my husband and I purchased a piece of property in the California desert. We were told it should be worth well over a hundred thousand dollars in about ten years or so. It was our retirement investment.

Here we are—over twenty years later—and while it very well may be worth that amount, we can't sell it. Why? Because there's an endangered bug living on it. I'm not sure what kind of bug it is, but evidently he's a big one because he needs all of our 5.5 acres to frolic in.

Don't get me wrong. I'm not saying there's anything wrong with saving a bug. I realize he's probably doing his part to keep the ecological system of our world intact. But couldn't we at least share the property? He could keep his half, and we'd sell off the other half. Sounds fair to me.

After all, why should he be entitled to the whole thing? He's not doing anything to help with the upkeep. He's not out there every Saturday pulling the weeds. He doesn't pay any taxes on it, or go to zone changing meetings. He's taking life easy. He's probably spending his days at the lake, sunning himself, hitching rides on jet skis, and only coming back to our land at night to sleep!

The reason I'm bringing up this matter at all, though, isn't to complain. It's to underscore the unpredictability of life. No matter how much we plan for the future, hope for the future, dream for the future, the bottom line is there aren't any guarantees. We have today. Appreciate it. Enjoy it.

## THOUGHTS TO PONDER

Can you honestly say that you've been living every day to the fullest?

How can you guard against wasting the here and now while you're dreaming and planning for tomorrow?

## BUMPER STICKER FOR THE DAY

> The best laid plans of mice and men
> often waste today.

## SCRIPTURE TO STAND ON

Do not boast about tomorrow,
for you do not know what a day may bring forth.

PROVERBS 27:1

## HELLO AGAIN, LORD...

Lord, help me to remember that the present is a present from you.

# SEVENTEEN
# Grand Opening

Are you afraid to be real? Do you hesitate to share your problems with anyone? That can be understandable if you've tried to be open in the past, but no one took the time to really hear you. We're all only human. After having our feelings ignored or trampled on, or our confidence broken time and time again, our natural instinct is to retreat, to protect our privacy, to hide our pain.

What would you say if I told you that you do have a friend to whom you can tell anything? And what if it didn't matter how bad or how stupid or how selfish you've acted? What if you were guaranteed that this friend would listen and, instead of being judgmental, be understanding and forgiving?

You already have a friend like that, but maybe you've been keeping him at a distance. Jesus is ready to give you all the comfort and encouragement you need, but maybe you're too afraid to take it. Maybe you're not ready to trust even him with your problems. If so, you're not letting him be the friend that you need—the only kind of friend he knows how to be.

Maybe it's time to change that, time to open up to a real friend.

## THOUGHTS TO PONDER

Have you ever confided something to someone and later regretted it?

Would you like to have a friend that you could tell anything to, one that you could trust with your feelings?

## BUMPER STICKER FOR THE DAY

> **We can't tell Jesus anything
> he doesn't already know.
> But he still likes hearing from us.**

## SCRIPTURE TO STAND ON

For a man's ways are in full view of
the Lord, and he examines all his paths.

PROVERBS 5:21

## HELLO AGAIN, LORD...

Lord, thank you that I can open up and be myself with you.

# EIGHTEEN

# The First Move

A friend of mine called the other day feeling down because one of his family members hadn't called in months and didn't seem interested in his well-being whatsoever. He was hurt because he had always been close to this family member in the past.

I listened for awhile, then told him to pick up the telephone and call him.

"No way," he said. "I'm always the one who calls. It's his turn now to call me."

He was right, of course. It was the other person's turn to call. But making the call wouldn't have been for his family member's benefit. It would have been for his own. He was the one who couldn't sleep at night. He was the one who was hurt over the situation. He was the one who would have gained the most by communicating.

Instead, my friend decided to go on harboring the hurt he didn't deserve, and feeling cheated out of a relationship he so desperately wanted. His refusal to make that first move was justified, but he was hurting the person who needed the situation healed the most. Himself.

## THOUGHTS TO PONDER

Is there someone in your life who you'd like to hear from?

What's keeping you from making that call?

## BUMPER STICKER FOR THE DAY

> Sometimes the most beneficial weightlifting
> we can do is with a telephone receiver.

## SCRIPTURE TO STAND ON

Hatred stirs up dissension, but love covers over all wrongs.

PROVERBS 10:12

## HELLO AGAIN, LORD...

Lord, for those relationships I truly want healed, help me not to just do "my part," but everything I can.

# ʃlip 'n ʃlide

As I write this, it's two days before Christmas and we're in the middle of an ice storm here in middle Tennessee. Having just moved here from Southern California, I'm not used to such things. I still need to mail some packages and do a little more Christmas shopping, but I'm following the advice of the Weather Channel and not venturing out onto the slippery roadways.

Christmas shopping is a good thing to do. But so is staying alive. Since the news is filled with scenes of multiple-car pileups and trucks that have slid off the road, I know I'm making the best decision between two good choices.

Throughout life, we're going to be faced with making a lot of decisions. Decisions between what's right and what's wrong are the easy ones to make. Granted, we might not always choose the right thing to do, but knowing what's right is usually pretty clear.

There are, however, times when we have to make a decision between two "right" things. The youth are going caroling at the senior's center and they need you to go. Unfortunately, that's the same night you promised your little brother you'd watch a video with him. You're also beginning to come down with a cold and don't think spending the evening outdoors would be very wise.

Both activities are good. Both would be pleasing to the Lord. But watching a video indoors and keeping your word to your little brother seems like the better thing to do. So you skip the caroling.

Instead of being applauded for using such wisdom, though, your friends accuse you of abandoning them. Your youth pastor says he really needed a strong soprano and you're the strongest one in the youth group. He tells you, quite frankly, that you let him down.

Keeping your word to your brother and taking care of your health was a good thing—but now you're starting to feel guilty about it.

Don't.

When we must decide between two good things, we should pray about it, then make our decision. Hopefully, it'll be the wisest decision. But by starting out with two good choices, you can rest assured that there won't be a wrong one.

## THOUGHTS TO PONDER

Can you recall a time when you had to make a decision between two right things? Write it down.

Which one did you decide to do? Why?

## BUMPER STICKER FOR THE DAY

> You don't get frequent flyer miles for going on guilt trips, so don't even board the plane.

## SCRIPTURE TO STAND ON

A heart at peace gives life to the body.

PROVERBS 14:30

## HELLO AGAIN, LORD ...

Lord, give me wisdom in all the choices I have to make today.

# TWENTY

# Tenderized

One of the secrets to Colonel Sanders' Kentucky Fried Chicken is the way it's prepared. Years ago, Colonel Sanders discovered that by using a pressure cooker, his chicken would turn out juicy and tender.

Pressure can make our spirits more tender, too. No, it's not fun having pressure in our lives. Most of us want a vent the size of the Grand Canyon—or better yet, escape the heat altogether. What we may not realize, though, is that those difficult times in our lives, the trials we wish would just go away, are the very things that are tenderizing us, making us more sympathetic to other people's pain and driving us closer to God.

Have you noticed that people who haven't gone through any real hardships in life usually can't handle the smallest crisis? They ask for prayer that they'll find the right color nail polish for a new outfit while others around them are requesting prayer for their parents who are getting a divorce, a boy at their school who was just shot in a drive-by shooting, or a sister recently diagnosed with leukemia.

None of us want to go through those difficult times of life, but if we trust the Lord through them, they'll make us better people.

## THOUGHTS TO PONDER

Have you had to face some tough times in life?

In what way do you think this trial has changed or will change you for the better?

## BUMPER STICKER FOR THE DAY

> **When the going gets tough,
> the tough know who to lean on.**

## SCRIPTURE TO STAND ON

If you falter in times of trouble,
how small is your strength!

PROVERBS 24:10

## HELLO AGAIN, LORD...

Lord, I may not always understand the trials I have to face, but I understand good can come from them if I place my trust in you.

# TWENTY-ONE

## Packing

Each time I've moved—seven times throughout my life—I've carried the same things from house to house to house. The same pictures, the same books, the same stuffed animals, the same mementos, the same dishes, the same cookware—there are boxes and boxes of things that I just can't leave behind.

Some of us go through life carrying emotional baggage with us wherever we go, too. We move to a different town, a different state, or maybe even a different country thinking we're going to have a fresh start. We go to new schools and new churches, and make new friends. But the old baggage, the same baggage that's weighed us down year after year, comes with us.

No matter how new the surroundings, or how much we want to change, we can't truly have a fresh start until we start leaving the old hurts, the old grudges, the old ways behind.

Remember the TV show "Let's Make a Deal"? Imagine that your best friend chose door number one and won ... a brand new living room set! What would you think if your friend passed on it, and hung on to her ratty old sofa instead, just because it was comfortable?

It's like that with God. He offers us a brand new life when we come to him. But we have to let go of our old bags so our hands grab everything he's giving us.

## THOUGHTS TO PONDER

Have you found yourself carrying baggage from relationship to relationship?

What do you think you should do with your "old baggage"?

## BUMPER STICKER FOR THE DAY

God makes us a new person.
We're the ones who keep putting
on the same old clothes.

## SCRIPTURE TO STAND ON

Forsake the foolish, and live;
and go in the way of understanding.

PROVERBS 9:6, KJV

## HELLO AGAIN, LORD...

Lord, whenever I feel weighed down, remind me to check to see if I'm carrying things I don't need to be carrying.

## TWENTY-TWO
# Heart Trouble

When our youngest son was two years old, he had to undergo two major heart surgeries a month or so apart. Needless to say, it was one of the most difficult times of our lives. His heart defect was diagnosed as a *patent ductus* (a valve problem) and a *ventricular septal defect* (a hole in the heart).

According to his team of cardiologists, it didn't matter how healthy the rest of his heart was, if these two problems weren't corrected, our son's life was in danger. Without thinking twice, we agreed to the surgeries.

It was the right decision. Thanks to an excellent surgical team, and a lot of prayer, today he's twenty-two years of age and doing fine. He still gets regular checkups every year, but his doctor is quite pleased with his progress.

Do you know God wants us to have regular checkups of our spiritual hearts, too? Just like our human heart, it doesn't matter whether or not most of it is working properly. It only takes one or two defects to put us at serious risk. Those defects can be corrected, though, with a thorough diagnosis, the proper care, and the right Physician.

## THOUGHTS TO PONDER

Are there some areas of your heart that need to be corrected?

Why do you think it's important for us to let God take care of any defects in our heart?

## BUMPER STICKER FOR THE DAY

If Jesus isn't taking up all of your heart, is he taking up any of it?

## SCRIPTURE TO STAND ON

Above all else, guard your heart,
for it is the wellspring of life.

PROVERBS 4:23

## HELLO AGAIN, LORD...

Lord, help me to follow your orders when it comes to the condition of my heart.

# TWENTY-THREE
## Winner's Circle

**D**o you know people who always have to win? If they don't win first place in a beauty contest, they accuse the judges of cheating, then trip the winner as she walks by. If they get an "F" on a history exam, they keep the teacher after school challenging each one of the answers. ("The War of 1812 did too take place in 1926!") Losing is not an option. No matter what the cost, no matter who they have to accuse or trample in the process, they're determined to win!

Obviously, people like this haven't realized the benefits of losing. The Bible is full of stories of people who had to lose before they won, but because they kept the faith and didn't give up, their victory turned out even better than they could have imagined.

Joseph was one of those people. Joseph had what it took to be a winner, but he also had some very jealous brothers. When he made the mistake of telling his brothers about some of his dreams, dreams that seemed to indicate that one day they might be serving Joseph, they got pretty ticked off. They threw him into a pit and planned to kill Joseph, telling their father that Joseph had been eaten by a wild animal. Then the caravan bound for Egypt came by, and they decided to sell him into slavery instead.

From the bottom of that pit, while working as a slave in Egypt, and later, after having been falsely accused and imprisoned, I'm sure it looked to Joseph as though he had lost, and lost big. But wait—look what happened next. Joseph, through a series of incredible events, ended up being released from prison and promoted to second in command over all of Egypt!

Imagine it—from a prisoner to second in command! From a major loss to a major win!

Even Joseph's brothers had to admit he was a winner. When famine hit, they had to stand before Joseph to beg for grain. Joseph's dreams had indeed come true, but did Joseph gloat over the situation? No. He forgave his brothers and gave them all the grain they needed.

So, don't ever think losing makes you a loser. In some instances, it's the best way to prove you're a winner!

## THOUGHTS TO PONDER

Why do you think it hurts to lose?

If God sees us as winners, how should that make us feel?

## BUMPER STICKER FOR THE DAY

> **Losing doesn't make you a loser.
> Giving up does.**

## SCRIPTURE TO STAND ON

Evil men do not understand justice,
but those who seek the Lord understand it fully.

PROVERBS 28:5

## HELLO AGAIN, LORD...

Lord, help me to remember that since you've made me a winner, nothing anyone can do or say can make me a loser.

# TWENTY-FOUR

## Stuck

I used to attend a church that had a parking lot that was partially unpaved. If you parked there during good weather, everything was fine. But if your car was parked in the dirt during a rainstorm, you could have quite a time trying to get it out of the mud. (Frankly, I think it was the pastor's way of making sure everyone stuck around for the Sunday evening service!)

One cloudy Sunday morning I made the mistake of parking in the unpaved part of the lot. It wasn't raining when I went into the church, so I thought I was safe. By the time I came out, though, it was pouring! I tried and tried to get my car moving, but it was stuck in about six inches of mud. The more I pressed on the accelerator, the deeper it got.

One by one church members walked by, offering their assistance. They tried pushing it out, pulling it out, even praying it out, but it wasn't budging. The prayer, though, did give one deacon enough wisdom to just tie a rope to the rear of his truck, tie the other end to my car, and tow me out.

Sometimes we can be like that car. We get ourselves stuck in situations that look perfectly fine at the moment, but the next moment they can become a muddy mess. If we're not too deep in the mud, we might be able to get out all by ourselves. If we're a little deeper, we might need our family, friends, pastor, or youth pastor to come along to pray or pull us out. And if we are really stuck, we just might need God to show up with a tow truck.

## THOUGHTS TO PONDER

Are you "stuck" in a situation that you've been trying to get out of all by yourself?

Do you think it might be time to get a little help?

## BUMPER STICKER FOR THE DAY

Not all mud baths are for our good.

## SCRIPTURE TO STAND ON

Do not set foot on the path of the wicked
or walk in the way of evil men.
Avoid it, do not travel on it;
turn from it and go on your way.

PROVERBS 4:14, 15

## HELLO AGAIN, LORD...

Lord, when I can't find a way out, help me to look up.

## TWENTY-FIVE

# Fly-By

On the night we taped the "Bob Hope—The First Ninety Years" television special, there was a preshow outdoor celebration in front of NBC. Hosted by Jay Leno, there were numerous civic leaders, celebrities, excited fans, and even a marching band on hand to congratulate Bob on his ninetieth birthday. We even brought our youth group down to celebrate the event.

One highlight of the festivities was to be a military "fly-by." When someone finally spotted the planes, we all watched with great anticipation as they flew toward us. Our hearts were pounding. Cameras were at the ready. People were pointing and cheering, cheering and pointing. The planes flew closer and closer and closer until....

Hey, wait a minute! Why are the planes flying over those other buildings? They're supposed to be flying over NBC! The audience erupted in laughter. The planes had missed us altogether. Jay Leno quipped something like, "Ladies and gentlemen, we've just bombed Burbank."

Not giving up, the pilots turned around and went back to make another pass. Again, we all watched their impressive approach. Closer and closer and ... you guessed it, they missed us again!

We all miss the mark at times. No matter how well we've trained, no matter how many times we've done the right thing, we can still miss. Anyone who tells you they hit the target every time hasn't been keeping a very accurate flight log.

The good news is that, when we miss our mark, God doesn't take our "wings" away. He just lets us turn around and try it again. And again. And again ... until we eventually get it right.

## THOUGHTS TO PONDER

Are there some areas in your life where you keep missing the mark?

When we miss the mark, do you think God wants us to give up or try again?

## BUMPER STICKER FOR THE DAY

> If we keep God in our sight,
> we'll never miss the mark.

## SCRIPTURE TO STAND ON

The path of the upright is a highway.

PROVERBS 15:19

## HELLO AGAIN, LORD...

Lord, when I miss the mark, help me to not give up, but have the courage to try again.

# TWENTY-SIX

# Snap!

**M**ost things break because they can't bend. Simple as that. Look at a tree the next time a storm passes through your area. The branches that have broken off are the ones that weren't able to bend with the wind. Being able to bend with the winds of life keeps us from breaking, too.

If our best friend is about to move away, we may cry and pray that it doesn't happen. But if it does, you have to be able to bend with the wind.

If our parents sit us down one day and tell us they're getting a divorce, it can feel as though we've been hit by a hurricane-force wind. But if we don't bend with that change in our lives, we'll break.

Bending with the winds of change doesn't mean we have to like or even approve of what is happening to us. I'm sure a tree would rather do without wind. It has to stand in it day in and day out, getting blown this way and that way, losing all its leaves in the process. But if that tree had to choose between bending with the wind or breaking in it, I'd guess it would much rather bend. In trees and people, bending means drawing on the strength of our roots, and guarantees that after the storm, we'll still be standing.

## THOUGHTS TO PONDER

Are you facing a major change in your life right now?

Have you been able to bend with the change or are you ready to break with it?

## BUMPER STICKER FOR THE DAY

> **The trouble with change is there's so much of it in life and so little of it in our pockets.**

## SCRIPTURE TO STAND ON

Whoever trusts in the Lord is kept safe.

PROVERBS 29:25

## HELLO AGAIN, LORD...

Lord, may the winds of life never uproot me.

# TWENTY-SEVEN

# Missing the Big Picture

There was a boy who desperately wanted to be on his church baseball team. He had some disabilities that slowed his movement and his reaction time, but none that slowed his enthusiasm. After some convincing, he was allowed to be on the team, but ended up spending most of his time on the bench. Why? Because the team had taken a vote to decide whether they wanted to win or just have a good time and let everyone play. They decided that winning was their goal, which basically meant everyone else ended up having a good time except this boy. Unfortunately, they weren't looking at the big picture.

My husband used to work with a program very much like the Boy Scouts. Whenever they had competitions, he made sure there was a category for every kid to win. If they were making race cars, there'd be a prize for the "Fastest," the "Best Blue," the "Best Red," the "Best Sanding," the "Best Numbers," and so on. There were a few people, though, who didn't agree with this thinking. They believed kids needed to learn what it's like to lose. (Ironically, these people were always the first to complain if it was their kid who didn't get a prize.)

My husband could never understand why anyone would complain that too many kids were turned into winners. Did they really think there was such a shortage of negative experiences in life that we had to make sure every kid had at least one? Obviously, these people weren't seeing the big picture either. Despite their criticism, my husband didn't change the way he ran the program. He thought it was his job to make sure the kids knew what it felt like to win.

We're all an accumulation of our hurts and joys, our wins and losses, time spent on the field and time spent on the bench. If we have the power to give someone a positive experience instead of a negative one, to help them feel good about themself instead of inadequate and inferior, what harm is that? It seems to me it's something Jesus would have done. He's making winners out of all of us ... in the big picture.

## THOUGHTS TO PONDER

Have you ever been cut from a team, or denied a chance to play in an activity? How did it make you feel?

Why do you think we so often place more importance on winning than on doing the right thing? Which do you think Jesus would want us to do?

## BUMPER STICKER FOR THE DAY

> **If God didn't want you on his team, why would he have paid such a high price for you?**

## SCRIPTURE TO STAND ON

Do not withhold good from those who deserve it, when it is in your power to act.

PROVERBS 3:27

## HELLO AGAIN, LORD...

Lord, thank you that you don't just look for the best players for your team, but the most trainable.

## TWENTY-EIGHT
# Unwanted Attachment

I recently went to dinner at a fine Italian restaurant with my son and his family. It was a fancy place where the dressing comes already on the salad instead of in a plastic packet. The food was great and we were having a wonderful time until the party at the table behind us got up to leave. On their way out, one of the men stopped by our table.

"I debated not saying anything," he said, "but if it was me, I'd want to know."

"Know what?" my son asked, puzzled.

The man leaned forward and whispered to my son, "You have a sucker stuck to your behind."

My son thanked the man for the embarrassing information, pulled the unwanted accessory off his pants, and we all had a good laugh. Who knows how long he had been walking around with the candy stuck to him like that? We had gone to church, walked around the mall, and walked the entire length of this restaurant, yet this man was the first person to let him know about it. Others may have noticed it, even talked or laughed about it among themselves, but no one bothered to tell him about it.

How often are we oblivious to the things we've allowed to attach themselves to our lives? Jealousies, unforgiveness, bitterness, anger, or gossip can be stuck to us just like that sucker, but we can't see them. It takes someone else to point them out to us, someone who truly cares about our welfare. When they do, we should listen. After all, they've got a better view of us than we do.

## THOUGHTS TO PONDER

Has a caring person recently pointed out some unwanted attachments that you might be carrying around with you?

Could that person be right? If so, what are you going to do?

## BUMPER STICKER FOR THE DAY

> Some of us can't see our problems even when we're sitting right on top of them.

## SCRIPTURE TO STAND ON

The way of a fool seems right to him,
but a wise man listens to advice.

PROVERBS 12:15

## HELLO AGAIN, LORD...

Lord, help me to listen more to those who care about my welfare, and heading that list is you.

# TWENTY-NINE
## Team Effort

Do you know your life is a team effort? It took two people to conceive you and, chances are, an entire medical team to bring you into this world. It takes a family to love and nurture you, a staff of teachers to educate you, a pastoral team to help guide you, friends to laugh and cry with you, garment workers to clothe you, farmers to feed you, firemen to let you know when dinner's ready (OK, that's just at my house). The list goes on and on. To put it simply, an awful lot of people have made some pretty big investments in your life.

Sometimes when you're down, you can feel like you're all alone in this world. Your emotions can tell you that no one cares. But that feeling has no basis in reality. How could it? It doesn't make sense when you consider how many people have already invested so much in your life. Maybe not all of them, but most of them want you to succeed.

And even if every single person in your life suddenly stopped caring about you, if every one of them turned his or her back on you, there's one friend who has promised to never ever do that—Jesus.

So, no matter what your emotions might be telling you at the moment, know that you're not alone. There are thousands of people who have invested in your life, and one Son of God. He made the biggest investment of all. So, you must be pretty special.

## THOUGHTS TO PONDER

Have you ever felt like no one cared? What made you feel this way?

Do you know someone who seems down lately? What can you do to show God's love to that person?

## BUMPER STICKER FOR THE DAY

> **No man is an island.
> But if he digs a defensive moat around himself,
> he can feel like one.**

## SCRIPTURE TO STAND ON

He who fears the Lord has a secure fortress,
and for his children it will be a refuge.

PROVERBS 14:26

## HELLO AGAIN, LORD...

Lord, when I'm feeling like no one cares, help me to remember how much you sacrificed to prove you do.

# THIRTY
# A Word From Our Maker

**A** friend of mine, Patty Freeman, recently sent me an e-mail that talked about a Fort Lauderdale advertising agency's recent billboard campaign. It was sponsored by an anonymous client and included such messages as:

*"Let's Meet at My House ... Sunday Before the Game"*
—God

*"What Part of 'Thou Shalt Not' Didn't You Understand?"*
—God

*"That 'Love Thy Neighbor' Thing, I Meant It."*
—God

*"Have You Read My #1 Best Seller? There Will Be a Test."*
—God

And my personal favorite ...

*"You Think It's Hot **Here?**"*
—God

Here are a few of my own ideas of what God might say if he really did have a billboard:

*"I created the world in six days.
The least you could do is clean your room in one."*
—God

*"I'll never leave you nor forsake you. But could you drive a little slower? Heaven's not ready for you yet."*
—God

*"Let go. It's my turn to carry your burdens."*

—God

*"Don't believe in me? Get real! I am."*

—God

*"Like earth? You haven't seen anything yet!"*

—God

## THOUGHTS TO PONDER

What do you think is the most important message that God wants to give to the world?

If you could write a billboard to God, what would it say?

## BUMPER STICKER FOR THE DAY

> **Sometimes when we're waiting for God to speak, he's waiting for us to listen.**

## SCRIPTURE TO STAND ON

Apply your heart to instruction
and your ears to words of knowledge.

PROVERBS 23:12

## HELLO AGAIN, LORD...

Lord, you don't need a billboard to speak to me. You've already written a pretty big book.

# THIRTY-ONE

# Home, Sweet Home

I once wrote a poem for a trucking magazine that I call my "Ode to Truckers." It went something like this:

*Truckin' 'cross America*
*seeing all she has to give.*
*I drive this rig from state to state*
*'cause I've forgotten where I live!*

Do you ever feel like that? Are you so busy going here and going there that it seems as though you've forgotten where you live? You can recall having a family once, and a bed, and maybe even a pet or two. But between school, basketball practice, swim team, and all your youth group activities, you don't have enough time left to breathe. As a matter of fact, breathing isn't listed in your "week-at-a-glance" calendar until 2:00 P.M. Wednesday.

Knowing how to carve time out of your schedule for yourself and your family is a skill you'll need throughout life, so you might as well learn how to do it now.

First of all, you have to understand a simple fact—there are twenty-four hours in a day. No more, no less. It doesn't matter how much time you need to get all your work done, you'll never be able to add another hour to the day or another day to the week. Every one of us is limited to living within the parameters of the calendar.

Second, you have to remember that your work, your friends, your youth group, your after-school clubs, aren't your family. Your family is your family. Certainly, God comes first in your life. Or at least he should. After that comes your family.

That may require saying "no" to some good people and worthwhile projects, but "no" isn't necessarily a bad word. It can save you a lot of grief in the long run. By saying no to insane schedules, you'll be saying yes to peace, yes to rest, and yes to being available for the things God really wants you to do.

## THOUGHTS TO PONDER

Do you "remember where you live"? Are you spending enough time with your family?

Why do you think it's important to maintain a healthy balance in our lives?

## BUMPER STICKER FOR THE DAY

> **The bee may be busy,
> but even he remembers he's got a hive.**

## SCRIPTURE TO STAND ON

Better a dry crust with peace and quiet
than a house full of feasting with strife.

PROVERBS 17:1

## HELLO AGAIN, LORD...

Lord, help me to manage my time better so I'll always have plenty for you.

# THIRTY-TWO

# One of a Kind

The recording artist Jewel recently had a hit song about kindness. Kindness—now there's a subject you don't see written about too much these days. There are songs written about gangs, violence, hatred, drugs, sexual innuendoes, disrespect, and just about everything else, but the word kindness doesn't turn up on too many lyric sheets.

But Jewel's right—kindness is important. Without kindness, no one would hold your place in line or open the door for you or help you pick up those two thousand straws you just knocked over at Taco Bell. No one would bring you a flower, tell you to have a nice day, or say "God bless you" when you sneeze.

Imagine what this world would be like if everyone suddenly stopped showing kindness: you ask your waiter for more soda and she tells you to get up and get it yourself. You ask your best friend to hold your jacket while you tie your shoe, and he says no, drops it in a rain puddle, and walks away. That store clerk, the one who's usually so nice, hands you your package and tells you to have "whatever kind of day you feel like having, just don't bother me again."

I don't think any of us would want to live in a world like that. That's why we have to do our part to keep the wheel of kindness turning.

Show a little kindness to someone today.

## THOUGHTS TO PONDER

How does it make you feel when someone shows kindness to you?

What can you do today to show a little kindness to someone?

## BUMPER STICKER FOR THE DAY

> Kindness is like a cold.
> If you don't keep passing it along,
> it'll eventually just go away.

## SCRIPTURE TO STAND ON

A kind man benefits himself.

PROVERBS 11:17

## HELLO AGAIN, LORD...

Lord, help me to be kind to the people I meet today, so that the people I meet tomorrow might be kind to me.

# THIRTY-THREE

# No Foolin'

**R**ather than simply talk about honesty, I thought for this particular devotional I'd include a crossword puzzle for you to complete before moving on with the rest of the book:

## Across

1. where people usually take an oath
4. _____ or consequences
5. honesty is the best _____

## Down

2. a president who was known for his honesty
3. when someone goes by another name

Crossword puzzles are fun, aren't they? They give us a clue, then it's up to us to figure out the right word and write it in the appropriate spaces. If you tried to do the puzzle on the previous page, though, by now you know that all the clues are wrong. The real clues are:

### Acro∬

1. to give a false impression
4. in old Westerns, what Indians say liars speak with
5. to make up a story

### Down

2. an untruth
3. to stretch the truth

Now, try it again. It should be a lot easier with the right clues. Hopefully, this little exercise didn't cause you too much aggravation, but it proves a good point. Honesty really does matter.

*Answers on Page 190

## BU(I)PER STICKER FOR THE DAY

> It'∫ no puzzle—
> hone∫ty really i∫ the be∫t policy.

## SCRIPTURE TO STAND ON

Food gained by fraud tastes sweet to a man,
but he ends up with a mouth full of gravel.

PROVERBS 20:17

## HELLO AGAIN, LORD...

Lord, help me to be honest with those around me, and most of all with you.

# THIRTY-FOUR

# Lining Up

Remember when you used to color in a coloring book and your mother or father would tell you to "stay within the lines"? It was important to stay within the lines because, if you didn't, your figures could end up with huge eyes, two heads, and legs coming out of their ears. (It kind of makes you wonder what Picasso's parents used to tell him, doesn't it?)

Remember when you first played T-ball and you had to learn to stay within the baseline? If you detoured by the snack bar on the way to first base, you'd be called out.

And what about when you first tried writing your name? I'm sure your teacher told you to "stay within the lines." It may have been hard at first, but before long those boundaries became second nature to you.

Now that you've outgrown coloring books and T-ball, and you know how to write your own name, it's still important to stay within the lines—the boundary lines that God has set forth in his Word. Those lines weren't meant to restrict you. They were meant to protect you, to help you make it safely around the bases, and to make sure that the picture of your life isn't confused and distorted, but turns out to be a real work of art.

## THOUGHTS TO PONDER

Are there some of God's boundary lines that you've been crossing over lately?

Why do you think it's important to stay within God's "lines"?

## BUMPER STICKER FOR THE DAY

> God gave us his commandments with the same love that he gave us his Son.

## SCRIPTURE TO STAND ON

He who seeks good finds goodwill,
but evil comes to him who searches for it.

PROVERBS 11:27

## HELLO AGAIN, LORD...

Lord, thank you for your laws, for they are only for my good.

# THIRTY-FIVE

# You Just Never Know

There was a popular song when I was young called "Patches." It was one of those songs that should come with the warning, "Caution: Listening to this song may be hazardous to your tear ducts." "Patches" told the story of a girl who wore clothes with patches and had a boyfriend whose family wouldn't let him see her because she was so poor. It was a modern-day Romeo and Juliet story.

My cousin Lynn and I used to listen to that song over and over and make our way through an entire box of tissues. Listening to "Patches" was a very special preteen memory for me because I didn't get to share many more songs with Lynn. She died shortly thereafter.

Now fast forward to today—since moving to Nashville, I've met a lot of wonderful people. One couple is Katie Brooks Lee and Dickey Lee. Katie recently invited me to a taping of a television special being produced by Larry Black. Larry was reuniting a group of rock 'n rollers from the 50s and 60s, and since her husband Dickey was in the Songwriter's Hall of Fame, he was a big part of the special.

From backstage Katie and I watched and listened with excitement as entertainer after entertainer told stories of their career, sang their hits, and shared their faith. Often, there wasn't a dry eye in the place.

Then it was Dickey's turn. Dickey shared a few wonderfully funny tales about his life as a singer and songwriter, then it was time for him to sing. As he started the first few lines of "Patches," my mouth dropped open.

"Dickey wrote that song, too?" I asked Katie, impressed.

"He didn't write it. He sang it," she said. "It was one of his hits."

I sat in amazement as Dickey sang the rest of that very familiar song. Who would have thought that the person responsible for some of my most cherished memories would one day be my friend? I only wish my cousin had been there to share it with me.

You just never know what life is going to bring your way. So if things don't seem very exciting right now, hold on. Only God knows what wonderful moments he has waiting for you!

## THOUGHTS TO PONDER

Who do you hope to meet someday?

Is there a particular goal that you'd like to accomplish sometime in your lifetime?

## BUMPER STICKER FOR THE DAY

> Life is like the movies.
> It's the parts we don't know are coming
> that bring us the most excitement.

## SCRIPTURE TO STAND ON

The house of the righteous contains great treasure.

PROVERBS 15:6

## HELLO AGAIN, LORD...

Thank you, Lord, for the life you've given me. I will look forward to each day with anticipation.

## THIRTY-SIX

# Up and at 'Em

No matter what happy greeting or Top Ten tune our alarm clock plays, there aren't many of us who enjoy being awakened first thing in the morning. Prying our eyes open and greeting the rising sun with "This is the day that the Lord hath made, let us rejoice and be glad in it" isn't always the first thought that comes to mind.

Most of us would rather just say, "This is the day that the Lord hath made. Wake me up when it's over." We don't have the energy to start our day with a groan, much less a smile. And morning devotions? You've got to be kidding!

Reading your Bible and spending time with God is good whenever you can do it, but do you know it's especially beneficial first thing in the morning? It gets your day off to the right start. It gets you focused, gives you strength for whatever you're going to face that day, and reminds you that you're loved. Can you think of a better way to start out your day?

This is the day that the Lord hath made, so let us rejoice and be glad in it.... Well, maybe after we hit the snooze button just one more time.

## THOUGHTS TO PONDER

How do you greet each morning?

What benefits do you think you could receive by setting aside five or ten minutes each morning to spend time with the Lord?

## BUMPER STICKER FOR THE DAY

> **When someone asks what state you live in, comatose is not the right answer.**

## SCRIPTURE TO STAND ON

I love those who love me,
and those who seek me find me.

PROVERBS 8:17

## HELLO AGAIN, LORD...

Help me, Lord, to be thankful for every day you give me ... even the mornings.

# THIRTY-SEVEN

# Empty Nails

**D**uring the earthquake in Northridge, California, practically every picture on the walls of our house fell down. Dozens of them. They had been hanging there for years, but after just thirty-five seconds of my house swing dancing on the faultline, my pictures were reduced to a pile of broken glass and bent frames.

With the thousands of aftershocks that followed, I decided to take my time hanging the photos back up. After all, why should I go to all the trouble of reframing them, only to have them hit the ground again in a five-pointer? It may have looked strange to have all those empty nails sticking out of the wall, but common sense is common sense.

When we finally did decide it was safe to go ahead and start rehanging things, I had a choice to make. I could hang up the same old photographs or I could start over with a whole new collection.

I opted to start over.

Do you know when we come to the Lord, he gives us a chance to start over, too? Maybe the earth won't move under our feet, shaking off our old habits and past mistakes, but the Bible does promise that all those old images of who we used to be will come down, leaving just the empty nails, ready and waiting to hold the "pictures" of our brand new life in him.

## THOUGHTS TO PONDER

Do you keep rehanging your past "pictures" of who you were, or are you showing the world a new you?

Why do you think God calls us a "new creation" in him?

## BUMPER STICKER FOR THE DAY

> **You can't have a new beginning until you let go of the past.**

## SCRIPTURE TO STAND ON

The fear of the Lord is a fountain of life,
turning a man from the snares of death.

PROVERBS 14:27

## HELLO AGAIN, LORD...

Lord, help me to forget my past and live for you today, so that I can look forward to my future.

# THIRTY-EIGHT
# Those Lazy Days of Summer

The Book of Proverbs talks a lot about laziness. King Solomon must have caught a few of his guards sleeping on the job, or had some teenagers who wouldn't take out the trash around the castle or clean the moat.

The wise ol' King was right. Laziness isn't an attribute that we should list on a job application. But then again, lazy people don't fill out too many job applications.

"I'm not working for minimum wage," they whine as they ask you for twenty bucks—a large chunk of the paycheck from *your* minimum wage job last Saturday.

"I can't find a job," they complain, holding a church bulletin that contains an ad for someone to help with gardening.

This type of person prefers letting others pay their way, and offers every justification in the book why that's OK. Sometimes they'll even try to make you feel guilty for earning money. "Can you pick up the tab this time—you know, since you've got a job and I don't?"

Now, I'm not talking about someone with a legitimate reason for not earning their own spending money. I'm talking about someone who is fully capable of working, has their parents' permission to work, and needs the money—but refuses to earn it. Lazy teenagers often make lazy adults, continuing to let others pay their way throughout their life.

So, be responsible. If you have some spare time over the summer, your grades are good, and your parents have been hinting for you to get a job (like taping the "Help Wanted" ads to your pillow), why not go fill out a few job applications? Who knows—you just might find something you actually enjoy doing. Ummm … earning money doing a job you enjoy … now there's a plan!

## THOUGHTS TO PONDER
Why do you think the Bible addresses laziness?

Lately, do you think you've been more of a giver or a taker?

## BUMPER STICKER FOR THE DAY

> **There are many things to avoid in life.
> Work isn't one of them.**

## SCRIPTURE TO STAND ON
A sluggard does not plough in season;
so at harvest time he looks but finds nothing.

PROVERBS 20:4

## HELLO AGAIN, LORD...
Lord, on those mornings when I feel like throwing my alarm clock across the room, remind me that work is a blessing and a privilege.

# THIRTY-NINE
## Special People

When I was in high school, I had about a two-mile walk home every day. No, it wasn't in three feet of snow, like some parents will tell you. Southern California doesn't get a lot of snow.

One day, a boy asked if I'd mind if he walked with me. I'd seen him around campus and we exchanged a smile from time to time, but I didn't know his name. Not his real one anyway. I knew the name some of the other kids at school called him. He was kind of a loner, stayed to himself most of the time. Many of the kids considered him a geek. Maybe he knew that, and that's why he stayed to himself.

I remember wondering as we walked what those kids at school would say if they saw me with him. But I didn't think about that for very long. He was a nice kid and, quite frankly, I was enjoying the company.

We passed the time not really talking about much of any-thing—homework, teachers, our school's football team. We walked and talked and laughed. When we got about a block or so from my house, he told me good-bye then turned around and started heading in the opposite direction. I found out later that he had gone completely out of his way to walk with me that day. I guess he really wanted a friend.

When I arrived at school that next morning, someone told me that this boy (they used his nickname) had suffered a hem-orrhage in his brain during the night and had died.

All that day I couldn't get that boy out of my mind. Why had our paths crossed? Why didn't I realize how little time he had left?

None of us know when the people we meet day in and day

out will be called to meet their Maker. We don't know how much time we ourselves have left. One thing I do know, though. I'm glad I didn't let the opinion of others stand in the way of my spending time with a very special person. I'm glad we got to talk, laugh, and most of all, become friends.

I only wish I had done it sooner.

## THOUGHTS TO PONDER

Is there someone at your school who's being shunned or made fun of?

What do you think God would want you to do about it?

## BUMPER STICKER FOR THE DAY

Jesus was a friend to the unlovable and it didn't hurt his popularity.

## SCRIPTURE TO STAND ON

A man of many companions may come to ruin,
but there is a friend who sticks closer than a brother.

PROVERBS 18:24

## HELLO AGAIN, LORD...

Lord, show me someone who needs a friend today, and help me to be that friend.

# FORTY

# No Sale? No Wonder!

A few years ago my husband and I decided to sell a house that we owned in another state. We signed a listing agreement with an agent and waited for the offers to begin pouring in. After a month or so of no offers or response of any kind, we decided to call the realtor to ask how things were going.

"Terrific," she said. "No one's looked at the property yet, but as soon as they make an offer, I'm ready to close the deal."

That wasn't exactly what we wanted to hear. We wanted to know why no one had visited the property. It was in a nice neighborhood, priced right, and in good condition. We figured it was time to start asking a few questions.

"Do you think the 'For Sale' sign is big enough?" we asked.

"'For Sale' sign?" she laughed. "I don't use 'For Sale' signs. They just clutter up the view."

That sounded a little odd coming from a realtor, but we pressed on.

"Well, what about newspaper ads? Haven't your ads on the property been helping?"

"Ads?" there was that laugh again. "I don't use them either."

"Oh, I see," my husband said. "You're waiting to put all your effort into holding an open house?"

"Never had much luck with those," she sighed.

Now we were really baffled. No sign, no newspaper ads, and no open houses? How in the world was she planning on selling our property?

"I'm just waiting for the right buyer to come along," she said, "then I'll cinch the deal!"

Needless to say, the house didn't sell. Its listing was the best-kept secret in town.

I wonder how many of us are treating our faith like that. Are we "keeping God's ways" so furtively that no one even suspects us of being a Christian? Is our relationship with the Lord prominently displayed by the life we lead, or is it the best-kept secret in town?

## THOUGHTS TO PONDER
Do your friends know you're a Christian?

In what ways would you like to show more of Christ in your life?

## BUMPER STICKER FOR THE DAY

> **Are you a proud soldier in God's army or just one of his secret agents?**

## SCRIPTURE TO STAND ON
Now then, my sons, listen to me;
blessed are those who keep my ways.

PROVERBS 8:32

## HELLO AGAIN, LORD...
Lord, may my gratitude for your love be enough to share it with all I meet today.

# FORTY-ONE

# With Two You Get Eye Roll

I used to have a friend who never said anything bad about anyone. She didn't have to. She'd just roll her eyes whenever a certain person's name came up. It wasn't gossip, she figured. After all, she had her mouth under control. It was up to the rest of us to fill in whatever details we wanted to infer from her optical gymnastics.

What she was doing, though, was worse than gossip.

"See that girl over there?" she'd begin. "I can't repeat what I heard about her because that would be gossip, and of course, gossip is wrong; but (rolling her eyes) if I could tell you ..."

And on she'd go, rolling her eyes and planting suspicion about this person, and all the while thinking she wasn't breaking any of God's rules. She wasn't fooling anybody, though—least of all God. He knew exactly what she was doing.

When God's own hand writes out a warning about bearing false witness, when he dedicates scripture after scripture to the dangers of the tongue, I'd say he didn't mean for us to find a loophole in his law. We should be keeping our whole body under subjection to him. Even our eyes.

## THOUGHTS TO PONDER

Why do you think God doesn't want us giving false innuendoes about people?

How do you think God feels when we purposely hurt another person's reputation?

## BUMPER STICKER FOR THE DAY

If you're making an innuendo, innuendon't.

## SCRIPTURE TO STAND ON

The folly of fools is deception.

PROVERBS 14:8

## HELLO AGAIN, LORD...

Lord, help me to keep my eyes on you, and to think more about the messages they can send.

# FORTY-TWO

# Sharing

Do you have a friend who shares everything with you? If she's having a bad day, she'll happily share all of her complaints until you're having a bad day, too.

She shares her enemies, too. If she doesn't like someone, she'll freely give you all the reasons why you shouldn't like him or her, either.

Another friend of yours wouldn't think of hogging a bad attitude. He shares every negative comment that pops into his head, and keeps on sharing them and sharing them until you've got a bad attitude, too.

These friends are also quite generous when it comes to their fears. There you are, trying to walk by faith, and all they can talk about is how nothing has ever gone right for them.

They share their bad attitudes, their enemies, their fears, their doubts, and their negativisms. You know what the saying— misery loves company. Sometimes, though, don't you wish friends like this would be just a little more selfish?

## THOUGHTS TO PONDER

Do you have a negative person in your life?

How do you keep their negativism from rubbing off on you?

## BUMPER STICKER FOR THE DAY

> **A bad attitude—**
> **more contagious than the common cold.**

## SCRIPTURE TO STAND ON

Hope deferred makes the heart sick,
but a longing fulfilled is a tree of life.

PROVERBS 13:12

## HELLO AGAIN, LORD...

Thank you, Lord, for all the blessings you give to us each and every day. If only we'd see them.

# FORTY-THREE
## Side Trips

Several years ago my family and I took a trip to Colorado. My husband, who is of Native American heritage, brought along a cassette of authentic tribal music to play as we took a side journey through Navajo Nation.

It wasn't the kind of music you usually hear in a car with three teenage boys, but it did give the experience a sense of realism. We stopped at all the trading posts along the way, buying hand-crafted turquoise jewelry, blankets, moccasins, and whatever else caught our eye. After spending enough money to put three kids through college, we decided to put our VISA card away and head back to the main highway.

We hadn't gone very far when ...

"Did you see that?" my husband said, slamming on the brakes.

"See what?" I said, now covered in what was left of my Diet Coke.

"That sign," he said, backing up the car so I could get a better look.

"'Dinosaur tracks'?" I said, skeptically reading off the hand-made sign. "I think someone's having some fun with some very gullible tourists."

"But what if it's true?" he said. "What if it's true and we were this close to it, but didn't check it out. We'd never forgive ourselves." I assured him I'd forgive myself, but he turned down the dirt road anyway.

After a mile or so, we came to a man standing in the middle of the road, directing us to park. He gave us a personalized tour of several interesting tracks nearby. It turned out to be one of the highlights of our entire vacation. And we almost missed it.

We miss out on a lot of things in life because of our skepticism. "I'm not going to youth group Friday night. The special guest speaker doesn't sound very exciting." Or, "Youth camp? No one I know is going. I'd have a terrible time." Or, "No way am I going to read that entire novel for English class! I'll rent the video, or interview someone who knows someone who did read the book. With all that dependable information around, why do I have to read it myself?"

All too often we miss out on a terrific experience just because we talk ourselves out of giving it a try. Don't get me wrong. We should never experiment with things that are illegal, sinful, or harmful. But sometimes it pays to stretch beyond our comfort zone, to give ourselves permission to have a new adventure in life. Who knows—we just might enjoy it.

## THOUGHTS TO PONDER

Is there a new adventure waiting for you?

What do you think is keeping you from trying it?

## BUMPER STICKER FOR THE DAY

> **Don't let your life be filled with could'ves, should'ves, would'ves, but rather, tried its!**

## SCRIPTURE TO STAND ON

Wisdom reposes in the heart of the discerning.

PROVERBS 14:33

## HELLO AGAIN, LORD...

Lord .... give me the courage to step out and try new things when it's in my best interest to do so.

# FORTY-FOUR
## 'Fraid Not

As director of "The Comedy College" in Pigeon Forge, Tennessee, I make the three-and-a-half hour drive from my home several times a week. I'm a newcomer to the South, so along the road I'm always watching for tornadoes ... even when there's not a cloud in the sky.

One cloudy day, though, I did see something suspicious on Interstate-40 just outside of Knoxville. It was funnel-shaped and stretched all the way from the sky to the ground. I tried my best not to panic, but immediately started looking around for a ditch to hide in. As I did, though, I noticed that the other drivers were going along like they didn't have a care in the world. Trucks were zooming past me going about eighty miles per hour, heading right into harm's way.

The radio in my car wasn't working, so I had no way of knowing in which direction the tornado was traveling, or what danger I was in. So, I decided to keep going, too, staying right behind the trucks. Maybe they knew something I didn't.

My heart was pounding as I drove closer and closer to the funnel cloud. I wondered when the hail would begin, or the wind and rain, or something to warn us of the imminent danger. But the air was still. The only sign that anything was wrong was that looming funnel cloud.

It wasn't until I was almost parallel to the cloud that I realized why the truck drivers weren't pulling off the road. What appeared so threatening a few miles back turned out to be smoke coming from a factory. My funnel cloud was man-made.

From a distance many things in life can appear just as threatening as that "tornado" looked to me. They can seem too big for us to handle, too powerful for us to stand up to, and far too damaging for us to ever survive. If only we'd take a closer look before we pull off the road, we might find that they're not tornadoes at all. They might just be harmless old smokestacks.

## THOUGHTS TO PONDER
Do you have a fear that's keeping you from moving ahead?

Were you ever afraid of something that turned out to be nothing? Write it down.

## BUMPER STICKER FOR THE DAY

We listen to Jesus on so many other things, why not when he says, "Fear not"?

## SCRIPTURE TO STAND ON
Fear of man will prove to be a snare.

PROVERBS 29:25

## HELLO AGAIN, LORD...
Fear and faith are enemies. Help me, Lord, to always side with faith.

# FORTY-FIVE

# Delayed Reaction

Ever been in a really bad mood, but you didn't know why? On the Grumpy Scale, you're somewhere between "pit bull" and "Saddam Hussein after a root canal." You're barking at everyone you meet, and basically being a real pain in the neck. You haven't a clue why you're so grumpy. You just are.

Whenever you get to feeling that way, the best thing for you to do is back up. That's right, start retracing your steps, just like you would if you'd lost your locker key. Go all the way back until you find the source of your sour disposition. Was it something that happened this morning, last night, a week ago, last month, or on the playground back in kindergarten? If you go back far enough, you'll usually be able to pinpoint the specific event or person that upset you. Then it's easier to resolve the issue—and lose the mood.

I don't know why, but many of us would rather pass along our irritation than confront the real source of our bad disposition. If a store clerk is rude to us, we'll take our package and smile, then be rude to everyone else we meet for the rest of the day. If our brother or sister says something to hurt us, we'll snap at our friends, our parents, and even our dog.

But is that really fair? It's like France being attacked by Russia, then bombing Canada in retaliation. It simply doesn't make sense. So, the next time you're grumpy, take a moment to find out the real reason behind your attitude. You might be surprised to discover something you didn't think bothered you, really did. And once you do, you're that much closer to resolving the situation and becoming yourself again.

## THOUGHTS TO PONDER

Have you been grumpy lately?

What do you think is the real source of your irritation?

## BUMPER STICKER FOR THE DAY

> **If you're having a bad day,
> don't blame the sun.**

## SCRIPTURE TO STAND ON

Like a city whose walls are broken down
is a man who lacks self-control.

PROVERBS 25:28

## HELLO AGAIN, LORD ...

Lord, help me not to let unresolved issues of yesterday affect my
joy today.

FORTY-SIX

# A Funny Feeling

On a recent plane trip from Nashville to Los Angeles, I heard the stewardess announce that our in-flight movie was going to be a Leslie Nielsen film. I love comedies, so I eagerly paid the four dollars to rent a set of earphones, then settled back to watch it.

It was a very funny movie, but halfway through, Nielsen's character was approached by some strangers who addressed him in Japanese. He then answered them in Japanese. Obviously, the plot had taken an unexpected twist. I assumed Nielsen was now playing his twin brother, who had been raised in Japan. It was pretty funny at first, but then the English-speaking Leslie never came back.

I watched the other passengers to see their reaction, but they were laughing and carrying on like nothing was wrong.

Finally, after about twenty minutes of not understanding a single word anyone was saying, I decided to check things out for myself. Not even the worst comedy writer would drag a gag on this long, I figured.

To my embarrassment, I discovered that somehow I had inadvertently pressed the button on the control panel switching my controls from playing the English version to playing the Japanese one. The joke was on me. I corrected the problem, and was able to enjoy the rest of the movie in my native tongue.

It amazes me to think how long I sat watching that movie, even though I couldn't possibly follow along. I knew that I was missing out on plenty of laughs and a lot of the plot, all because I wouldn't follow my instincts and check the situation out for myself. And yet, I relied upon the reactions of the other passengers to determine whether or not everything was all right.

Are you handling life's problems that way? When you sense something's wrong, do you heed those inner warnings and check things out, or do you write it off as the pepperoni and sausage pizza you had last night for dinner? God gave us our instincts. It's a good idea to listen to them once in a while.

## THOUGHTS TO PONDER
Is there something in your life that doesn't "feel" right?

Why do you think you're feeling uneasy about this situation?

## BUMPER STICKER FOR THE DAY

**When in doubt, check it out.**

## SCRIPTURE TO STAND ON
Ears that hear and eyes that see—
the Lord has made them both.

PROVERBS 20:12

## HELLO AGAIN, LORD...
Lord, your Holy Spirit never talks unless he has something important to say. Help me to listen.

# FORTY-SEVEN

# A Master Juggler

It's fascinating to watch a juggler in action. How some of them can keep those bowling balls, torches, and chainsaws in the air and not end up in the emergency room is beyond me. I have a hard enough time handling just one chainsaw while slicing my roast beef at dinner time.

Life can sometimes make you feel like you're doing a juggling act. You work and train hard to get school, family, and church in the air at the same time.

Then, just when you think you're adequately handling those three facets of your life, someone comes along and tosses in friends. You manage to work in friends along with school, family, and church, but then a job gets added, and after-school sports, and maybe a mission trip. Somehow you find a way to juggle all of them, but you know it's just a matter of time before everything comes crashing down on top of you.

When God created us, he didn't intend for us to never take a break. He took one himself. Even if everything we're juggling is good, it's not his plan that we keep so many balls in the air, we can't even stop and talk to him for a moment. He wants us to live a balanced life.

Jesus did. He could have been holding rallies and healing people 24-7. But he didn't. He rested. So did the Father, when he created the world. If rest is important to God, how much more important should it be to us?

## THOUGHTS TO PONDER

How many things are you juggling right now?

What place have you given God?

## BUMPER STICKER FOR THE DAY

> **If you're trying to live the lives of six people, stop and check your I.D. again. There's only one of you.**

## SCRIPTURE TO STAND ON

Her ways are pleasant ways,
and all her paths are peace.

PROVERBS 3:17

## HELLO AGAIN, LORD...

Lord, help me not to overestimate my day and my energy.

# FORTY-EIGHT
# Mind Change

I change my mind a lot. You should see me in a parking lot looking for a parking space. I'll start to pull into one vacant space, then decide it's too tight and go on to another one. Then, just as I'm heading into that one, I'll decide the angle isn't right, back up, and drive to the next one. By the time I find one I like, the mall's usually closed.

I change my mind when deciding what to cook for dinner, too. Pot roast? No, I can't afford more dental work. Meatloaf? No, the family's still having recurring nightmares from the last one. After ruling out most of my other favorite recipes for life saving purposes, I usually decide to just take the family out to eat.

But that's OK. I'm allowed to change my mind.

Do you know you're allowed to change your mind, too?

If you've already said you'd go to that party Friday night, but now you're having second thoughts, it's perfectly all right to change your mind. In fact, that could be the Holy Spirit telling you it's not the sort of place you should be.

If you've already promised your best friend that she can copy your homework, but now you're starting to feel guilty, you can change your mind. If you do, she might actually learn something from the lesson, and in the long run, that's being a better friend.

So, when you agree to something and after thinking about it feel it's not the right thing to do, remember you can always change your mind. Of course, if you grow up to be an astronaut, I'd suggest doing it before lift-off. NASA might not be too happy to hear you say after only twenty seconds into flight, "All right, turn this baby around and take me home. If you've seen one galaxy, you've seen them all!"

## THOUGHTS TO PONDER

Have you ever wished you had changed your mind about something?

Did you have a feeling ahead of time that you should have changed your mind? Why do you think you didn't listen to that feeling?

## BUMPER STICKER FOR THE DAY

> **A decision isn't like Jesus.
> It's not unchangeable.**

## SCRIPTURE TO STAND ON

Let the wise listen and add to their learning,
and let the discerning get guidance.

PROVERBS 1:5

## HELLO AGAIN, LORD...

Lord, help me not to be afraid to change my mind when it needs to be changed.

# FORTY-NINE

# Waiting and Waiting and ...

**"W**e ordered that burger and fries over ten minutes ago. What's taking that waitress so long? Is she personally inspecting all the meat for mad cow disease?"

Wait. Wait. Wait. There are times when it seems like that's all we do. According to the Bible, sometimes that's all we're supposed to do.

When we ask the Lord for something, we usually want it NOW. We're convinced we need it NOW. We can't understand why he isn't giving it to us NOW. But God has his own timing, and his timing's perfect.

When my youngest son was facing his heart surgeries at two years of age, I learned a good lesson about God's timing. When the first surgery was scheduled, we asked the church to pray, then drove him to the hospital and checked him in. Upon examination it was determined that he had a slight temperature, so they cancelled the surgery and sent him home. The surgery was scheduled for the following week, but the exact same thing happened. This went on week after week after week.

Finally, I had a heart-to-heart with God about it. I told him that I didn't want my son to have surgery, but if he had to have it, then I really wanted to get on the other side of the crisis. I wanted it over with, the sooner the better.

The next time I took him to the hospital, I was confident things would go my way. They didn't. He had a slight fever again, and they sent him home.

*Maybe God misunderstood me,* I thought to myself. *Didn't he hear me when I said I wanted the surgery to be over with?* He had heard me, of course, but he also knew what was best for me.

That next week, a certain news item on television caught my eye. A reporter, standing in front of the hospital where my son was to have his surgery, said that one of the doctors in that hospital's pediatric ward had just been diagnosed with hepatitis. Any children who had been seen by him were being advised to return to the hospital for evaluation.

Since my son had only been seen by a nurse and sent home, he was spared the exposure to that terrible virus. I had no idea that danger was even in the equation when I was advising God about what to do. But God did.

God's timing is always perfect. When we pray, we should believe that God will answer our prayers in his perfect timing. We really wouldn't want our answers any sooner than that, anyway.

## THOUGHTS TO PONDER

Do you have a prayer that seems to be taking forever to be answered?

Why do you think God might not be answering it just yet?

## BUMPER STICKER FOR THE DAY

> **Trusting in God's timing will take care of your "wait" problem.**

## SCRIPTURE TO STAND ON

Trust in the Lord with all your heart,
and lean not on your own understanding.

PROVERBS 3:5

## HELLO AGAIN, LORD...

Lord, help me to be anxious for nothing, but to gladly wait on your timing.

# FIFTY

# Beaming With Pride

**P**ride. It's not always what we think it is.

Did you know that timidity can be pride? If our timidity is keeping us from standing up for our beliefs because we don't want to risk people rejecting us, then that timidity could be coming from a prideful place.

Boldness can be prideful, too. If we're so outspoken that we never stop to consider the validity of someone else's opinion, then our boldness is coming from a prideful place. We need to let other people get a word in edgewise.

Judging others, which on the surface can seem quite spiritual, is usually coming from a prideful place. The Bible warns us that if we want God to go lightly at our judgment, we need to go lightly on the judgment we hand out to others.

We all know that pride can easily enter into a rich man's heart, but even poverty can make us proud. Have you ever heard people brag about the things they don't have? I'm not talking about those with real needs; people with real needs often don't talk about them. I'm talking about people who enjoy complaining and whining about all the things they don't have—except a job. If they complained about that too much, someone might offer them work, and then what would they do?

Obviously, we can have pride in a lot of areas of life. That's why we have to pray for God to reveal those places where we battle pride, and help us not only to win the battle, but to fight it in the first place.

## THOUGHTS TO PONDER

Are there areas in your life where you might need to battle pride?

Why do you think pride can be so harmful to us and those around us?

## BUMPER STICKER FOR THE DAY

> **Pride, and loose shoelaces,**
> **cometh before a fall.**

## SCRIPTURE TO STAND ON

Do you see a man wise in his own eyes?
There is more hope for a fool than for him.

PROVERBS 26:12

## HELLO AGAIN, LORD...

Lord, remind me that when I walk in pride, it's easy to trip up.

# FIFTY-ONE

# Turned Away

**Y**ears ago, someone gave me tickets to a taping of a new TV show called "Mork and Mindy," starring the up-and-coming comedy star, Robin Williams. After waiting in line for more than two hours, the studio pages finally opened the doors and began letting in the overflow crowd of people, one at a time.

As the line inched closer and closer to the entrance, the more excited I became. I was a big fan of the show, and couldn't believe I might actually get to see Robin Williams in person.

Unfortunately, by the time I reached the front of the line, the theater was full. The very last person they allowed in was the man in line ahead of me. The page dropped his hand in front of me and said, "All right, this is the cutoff."

Getting turned away doesn't feel very good any time, but it especially doesn't feel good when you're that close. I was *so* disappointed. They handed me a "turnaway ticket," which meant I could come back and see the show at a later date (which I did), but I was still disappointed that night.

Being turned away for a television show taping is nothing compared to what it might feel like to get turned away from heaven. Imagine it—you're standing in line, peeking around the pearly gates trying to get a glimpse of the magnificence of the place, when someone turns to you and says, "Sorry, but everyone whose name was on the list has already checked in. The admission stops here." And just in case you're wondering, heaven doesn't hand out turnaway tickets. You only get the one chance. Be ready.

## THOUGHTS TO PONDER

How do you think it would feel to be turned away from heaven?

How do you think it would feel to watch your friends or family members being turned away?

## BUMPER STICKER FOR THE DAY

Jesus already bought your ticket to heaven.
It's up to you to take it with you.

## SCRIPTURE TO STAND ON

Leave your simple ways and you will live;
walk in the way of understanding.

PROVERBS 9:6

## HELLO AGAIN, LORD...

Lord, thank you for purchasing my ticket to heaven through your death on the cross. I can never pay you back, or thank you enough.

# FIFTY-TWO
## Cheap Shot

Who do you think of when you hear the word "classy"? I think of Bob Hope. In all the years I wrote for him, I never heard him kick a person while he was down. It would have been easy to do—a person who hits bottom all too often becomes the subject of cruel jokes. But if a person was truly going through a crisis—for example, if someone had made all the major newspapers because of alcohol dependency—Bob would leave the entire incident alone. As far as he was concerned, the person needed help, not teasing.

When we hear about someone messing up, our human tendency is to laugh at their situation or mock their bad judgment. In some ways, it probably makes us feel better about ourselves. If you don't think that's true, wait until the next publicized scandal or tragedy and see how fast the jokes start rolling.

That's not to say there aren't plenty of items in the news and in life that we can't help but laugh at. There are. But when it comes to people's genuine health or emotional problem, when their lives and their families are already in turmoil, shouldn't we be laughing at things they can laugh at, too?

## THOUGHTS TO PONDER

Why do you think we shouldn't kick someone when they're down?

How do you want to be treated when you fail?

## BUMPER STICKER FOR THE DAY

> Laugh at someone else's calamities,
> and they'll buy the first ticket
> to laugh at yours.

## SCRIPTURE TO STAND ON

The desire of a man is his kindness.

PROVERBS 19:22, KJV

## HELLO AGAIN, LORD...

Lord, help my laughter to not come at the expense of someone else's joy.

# FIFTY-THREE
## No Passing Zone

**H**ave you ever had a friend who was there for you through thick and thin—until you started to move ahead of him or her? When you were both trying out for the cheerleading squad, she was giving you all sorts of pointers. When you both signed up for the basketball team tryouts, he'd shoot hoops with you every night.

Then, when you made the finals and your friends didn't, all of a sudden that "free advice" turned into criticism. Maybe they even encouraged you to drop out of the competition altogether. "You'll never make it," they said. "You might as well just go ahead and bail."

Before you blindly follow their advice, it might be a good idea to first analyze where that advice is coming from. Are you hearing sound wisdom or simply the voice of jealousy? Are they genuinely trying to help you or are they just making sure you don't pass them up?

True friends will be happy with your accomplishments. They might be disappointed, of course, if they don't make the finals while you do, but they wouldn't dream of doing anything to sabotage your chances of making the team.

So, be careful whose advice you listen to. Just because it's coming from your friends, you still need to make sure it's coming from a friendly place.

## THOUGHTS TO PONDER

Has anyone ever given you "unfriendly" advice?

What do you think motivates someone to keep another person from reaching his or her dreams?

## BUMPER STICKER FOR THE DAY

> **Advice is like fruit.**
> **You have to look at it from all angles**
> **to make sure it's good.**

## SCRIPTURE TO STAND ON

Wounds from a friend can be trusted,
but an enemy multiplies kisses.

PROVERBS 27:6

## HELLO AGAIN, LORD...

Dear Lord, when it comes to good advice and bad advice, grant me the wisdom to know the difference.

# FIFTY-FOUR

# Truth or Dare

**H**ave you ever played a game called "Truth or Dare"? When it's your turn, you choose between telling the truth about a personal question—or taking a dare. Sometimes the game is harmless, other times it's not. You may discover that playing this game can jeopardize your reputation—or your health.

When someone dares you to do something—as part of a game or in any other context—he or she isn't always thinking about the outcome, so you'd better. It's your life and your reputation. Your friends' entertainment shouldn't have lasting consequences on your life.

If you're the type of person who likes to accept dares, at least set wise standards for the ones you agree to or the "dangerous truths" you choose to tell. Don't do or say anything that isn't in your long-term best interest. There are some dares that are perfectly safe, though. Dare to trust God with your problems, knowing that he wants the very best for you 100 percent of the time. Dare to follow his ways and be all you can be in him. Then you'll be playing the game God's way, and only good can come of that.

## THOUGHTS TO PONDER

Have you ever accepted a dare that you wish you hadn't?

Were the consequences or risk you took worth it?

## BUMPER STICKER FOR THE DAY

> **When God gave us brains,
> it wasn't just for filler.**

## SCRIPTURE TO STAND ON

Preserve sound judgment and discernment.... Then you will go on your way in safety, and your foot will not stumble.

PROVERBS 3:21a, 23

## HELLO AGAIN, LORD...

Lord, help me to act responsibly with the life you've given me.

# FIFTY-FIVE

# I've Got Everything Under Control ...

Feeling a little stressed? Many of life's stresses come from thinking that our earthly journey is supposed to be trouble-free. When our carefully crafted plans don't materialize, when circumstances take us in a direction we hadn't counted on, when we're hit in the face with problems we didn't see coming, we get stressed.

If life is anything, it's unpredictable. If you're feeling like you're on top of a mountain today, tomorrow you could look down and realize you've been standing on a volcano all along. Just because things are going well right now is no guarantee they'll stay that way.

Or to look at it another way, if nothing seems to be going right in your life today, you can almost bank on the fact that something wonderful is just around the corner. That's life. It's how it's supposed to be. Heaven is where we're guaranteed no troubles. Not here.

We keep trying to make life work differently. We think we're supposed to be in control of our circumstances at all times. When things go wrong, we automatically assume we've lost that control and failed. That's why we get stressed. But we're not supposed to have everything under control. God is. And he does. So relax.

## THOUGHTS TO PONDER

Has your life seemed out of control lately?

Why do you think it's better to let God have control of our lives?

## BUMPER STICKER FOR THE DAY

> We wouldn't think of asking a pilot
> to scoot over so we could fly the plane
> for a while. Why do we do that with God?

## SCRIPTURE TO STAND ON

The righteous will never be uprooted.

PROVERBS 10:30

## HELLO AGAIN, LORD...

Lord, help me to trust your navigational skills and leave the flying to you.

# FIFTY-SIX

# True Riches

When my husband was growing up, he and his family lived in a one-car garage adjacent to his aunt's house. They had to take showers in an outdoor makeshift stall, which used the cold water from the garden hose. The garage was eventually condemned by the city and had to be torn down, but to this day he can remember the icy showers and the sound of the cockroaches scurrying under the crate that he stood on while showering.

One Christmas he received a note from Santa stuffed into the sock that he had hung on their stove. In his mother's writing it said, "I delivered toys to all the other poor boys and girls and ran out. Sorry. Love, Santa."

It's hard to trust God when you don't have a lot of money, when you're wondering where your next meal is coming from, or when there aren't any presents under the Christmas tree ... again. But my husband will be the first to admit that even though he didn't get everything he wanted during those lean years, God provided everything he needed.

We've learned a lot about God's faithfulness throughout our marriage, too. We've had both prosperous times when money was no object and times when we didn't know how we were going to make our next house payment. Whichever situation we found ourselves in, God was always faithful. Not once. Not twice. But every single time there was a need.

When God promised in his Word never to fail us, he wasn't kidding. It doesn't matter how much money is in our savings account, or whether or not we get that designer jacket, the bottom line is God will meet every one of our needs. Not our wants. Our needs. And knowing that truth make us all millionaires!

## THOUGHTS TO PONDER

Do you wish you had more money?

What does it mean to say God's faithfulness is worth more than riches?

## BUMPER STICKER FOR THE DAY

> **Compared to God's net worth,
> Bill Gates is a pauper.**

## SCRIPTURE TO STAND ON

Better a poor man whose walk is blameless
than a rich man whose ways are perverse.

PROVERBS 28:6

## HELLO AGAIN, LORD...

Lord, thank you for not granting all of my desires, but for always meeting my needs.

# FIFTY-SEVEN

# Here Comes the Judge

How good of a judge are you? Do you make a judgment after listening to only one side of a story, or do you wait and get all the facts first?

My grandmother, Ella, was an avid "Perry Mason" fan. She watched so many episodes, she could probably pass the bar exam. Today, shows like "L.A. Law," "Law and Order," and "Murder, She Wrote" turn us into amateur sleuths. We often figure out the perpetrator's identity before the second commercial break.

But that's television. The clues are scripted for us and we're given all the necessary facts. In reality, it's much harder to correctly judge another person's actions, to discern who's telling the truth and who isn't, whose alibi holds water and whose leaks like a sieve. An experienced truth bender can come off looking quite innocent, while a nervous, stammering witness can lose all credibility no matter how honest he or she is being.

God warned us about judging others. Of course, we have courts for legal matters, but I'm referring more to the judgment we so often pass on those around us. God knew we wouldn't take the time to gather all the facts. He does. He knew we can't correctly determine the motives of another person's heart. He's an expert at it. He knew we'd be wrong in our judgments more often than not. That's why he took the job, instead of giving it to us.

## THOUGHTS TO PONDER

Has someone ever incorrectly judged you? How did it make you feel?

Why do you think it's important that we leave the judging to God?

## BUMPER STICKER FOR THE DAY

> **Only the Lord can judge others because only he was willing to die for them.**

## SCRIPTURE TO STAND ON

A man's wisdom gives him patience;
it is to his glory to overlook an offense.

PROVERBS 19:11

## HELLO AGAIN, LORD...

Lord, remind us that only you keep the record books, and that they don't need our auditing.

# FIFTY-EIGHT
## Life Signs

I magine what it would be like to drive around without any road signs. Twenty-car pileups at every intersection. No one would know when to watch for school children, merging traffic, ice, or falling rocks. We wouldn't know when the road's going to curve, dip, detour, or simply end.

Street signs are important. They tell us when men are working, and whether our speed is being checked by aircraft, radar, or if we're just on the honor system. Signs tell us whether we should stay to the right or to the left, where and when we can make a U-turn, and when we should use extreme caution (like when I'm out on the road).

Signs bring order to our journey and help keep us on the road and out of the ditch. They even tell us where to expect various livestock to cross the street. (Although why they can't cross with a crossing guard at the regular crosswalks like the rest of us is beyond me.)

Did you know God's Word gives directional signs for life? It tells us what to watch out for, when to make a U-turn, and when we're headed straight for a dead end. And just as road signs can bring order to our journey, the Bible can bring order to our lives.

So, if we're finding ourselves involved in a few too many emotional fender benders, if we're continually running God's red lights, making unsafe lane changes, or going off the road altogether and ending up in the ditch, maybe it's time we went back to the manual and brushed up on the rules of his road.

## THOUGHTS TO PONDER

Why do you think it's important to follow God's road signs?

List a few of God's "road signs" that you wish more of us would follow.

## BUMPER STICKER FOR THE DAY

> **The road to heaven is never a dead end.**

## SCRIPTURE TO STAND ON

Keep my commands and you will live;
guard my teachings as the apple of your eye.

PROVERBS 7:2

## HELLO AGAIN, LORD...

Thank you, Lord, for your Word. It's the best map on the market.

## FIFTY-NINE

# In Over My Head

When I was in my early twenties, I accepted a position as secretary of our church. I knew how to type, compose letters, take minutes in shorthand, and keep records. What I didn't know how to do was operate the mimeograph machine. (In those days before computers and copiers, it was either use the mimeograph machine or chisel it in stone.)

I had been working in my new position barely a week when the pastor informed me that the newsletter needed to be done. Embarrassed to confess that I didn't know the first thing about mimeographing, I assured him I'd have it done and mailed off by end of day. *It's just a mimeograph machine, not brain surgery,* I thought. *How hard could it be?*

Famous last words.

After sending hundreds of papers flying through the air and getting covered in so much black ink I looked like I'd gone swimming in the La Brea Tar Pits, I finally quit pretending I knew what to do. Sheepishly, I called Ginger Forester, a lady in the church who had been doing the newsletter for years. Within minutes she was at the church, eager and willing to help. She understood the panic I was going through because she had been in that position herself. She had learned, by trial and error, every aspect of that machine. Together, we met the end-of-day deadline for the newsletter.

Are you trying to tackle one of life's problems the same way I was tackling that newsletter? Have you told others and yourself that you can handle it, that you don't need any help? It's easy to get trapped into that kind of thinking.

Life comes with problems. They're inevitable. The good news is, we don't have to learn all our lessons the hard way. When you're faced with a particularly tough decision, pray about it, then go get yourself some good, godly counsel. It's those times when I didn't pray or seek good counsel that I've ended up with a lot of ink on my face.

## THOUGHTS TO PONDER

Do you have a problem that you've been trying to solve yourself?

Is there someone you know who could give you good counsel concerning your problem?

## BUMPER STICKER FOR THE DAY

Good advice—you can never overufe it.

## SCRIPTURE TO STAND ON

Plans fail for lack of counsel.

PROVERBS 15:22

## HELLO AGAIN, LORD …

Dear Lord, help me to remember the importance of seeking and listening to good counsel.

## SIXTY

# Don't Forget!

I love Post-it™ notes. My home is literally wallpapered with them. I've got a note in my office reminding me to finish this manuscript, a note by the phone reminding me to call a business associate, and one in my kitchen reminding me to check on dinner. (That last one's hard to read through all the smoke.)

Whether you use Post-it™ notes, memo pads, or strings tied around your fingers, it's good to remind yourself of the things you need to do throughout your day. Without some sort of memory jogger, it's too easy to forget those important tasks, errands, and homework assignments.

Sometimes I think it'd be a good idea to have memory joggers for applying the Bible to our lives, too. God's Word is full of wisdom on how to live our lives, but all too often we forget what it says. That's where a few Post-it notes might come in handy.

For instance, if a bully is picking on us at school, the Post-it™ in our locker might read, "When a man's ways are pleasing to the Lord, he makes even his enemies live at peace with him" (Proverbs 16:7).

And when we're dying to put someone in his or her place, we could just stick one over our mouth that says, "He who guards his mouth and his tongue keeps himself from calamity" (Proverbs 21:23).

A few of us might need to hang one on the headboard above our bed that says, "Laziness brings on deep sleep, and the shiftless man goes hungry" (Proverbs 19:15).

All of us could probably use one by our telephone that says, "Without wood a fire goes out, without gossip a quarrel dies down" (Proverbs 26:20).

You get the idea. God's Word is worth remembering. We should do whatever we need to do to make sure it sticks.

## THOUGHTS TO PONDER

Which of God's promises or laws do you have a difficult time remembering?

Why do you think it's important for us to remember what God's Word says?

## BUMPER STICKER FOR THE DAY

> **Why is it so easy to remember our problems and forget God's promises?**

## SCRIPTURE TO STAND ON

Every word of God is flawless;
he is a shield to those who take refuge in him.

PROVERBS 30:5

## HELLO AGAIN, LORD...

Lord, your Word is a lamp unto my feet. Help me to remember to use it.

# SIXTY-ONE

# And for My Next Number ...

Do you know that, early in his career, Walt Disney was told by an editor of a Kansas City newspaper that he'd never make it as an artist? But Walt Disney believed in himself and his talent and, of course, the rest is history.

Talent is subjective. One music teacher might tell you you're going to be the next Amy Grant, while another says your singing sounds more like Ulysses S. Grant. One coach might compare your golf swing to Tiger Woods and take notice, while another might just take cover. Your seventh-grade English teacher might have been totally blown away with your sense of dialogue and story. But your eighth-grade one might suggest you take up welding instead of writing.

So, how do you know if you really have talent?

You keep using it. Even the weakest muscles grow stronger from constant use. If you keep using your talent, you'll naturally improve. As time goes on, you'll learn how to assess your own level of skill. And, who knows? One day, you just might be the next Walt Disney.

## THOUGHTS TO PONDER

What do you feel are your strongest talents?

Why do you think it's important to believe in yourself and your talents?

## BUMPER STICKER FOR THE DAY

> Buried talents don't bring anyone any joy, least of all the person who buried them.

## SCRIPTURE TO STAND ON

All hard work brings a profit.

PROVERBS 14:23

## HELLO AGAIN, LORD...

Lord, I dedicate my talents to you, to use them as you see fit.

## SIXTY-TWO

# Rules and Reasons

Parents. Sometimes you just don't know where they're coming from, do you? One day they seem so supportive, and the next day they impose some rule on you that you just can't understand or deal with. They're not letting you dress the way you want, hang out where you want, or have the friends you want. What's with them anyway? Animals let their young wander off on their own shortly after they learn to walk. Why can't parents be more like animals?

Ever heard of roadkill?

Most parents establish rules for their children's protection. Contrary to what you might think, your parents want you to have fun, dress stylishly, and have plenty of good friends. But they've also invested an awful lot of love, energy, money, and time into you, and they're going to protect that investment. If they see you developing behaviors that will cause you harm in the long run, they're going to speak up. If they notice you're hanging around the wrong crowd, they're going to feel compelled to say something.

You can rebel, of course. That's your choice. But why would you want to, when all they're doing is loving you? They're your parents, not your enemies. You're all on the same team. Work together. They want you to turn out the very best you can. Isn't that what you want, too?

## THOUGHTS TO PONDER

Have you been having a difficult time understanding where your mother or father is coming from?

List some of your parents' rules and what you think might be their reasoning behind them.

## BUMPER STICKER FOR THE DAY

> Communication is like a campfire.
> Everyone could warm up
> if someone would just start it.

## SCRIPTURE TO STAND ON

There are those who curse their fathers
and do not bless their mothers.

PROVERBS 30:11

## HELLO AGAIN, LORD...

Lord, help me to understand my parents the way I want them to understand me.

## SIXTY-THREE

# Winning the Gold

When the Olympics came to Los Angeles, we tried to get tickets to several of the events, but by the time we mailed in our order, they were all sold out. Still wanting to be a part of history, we drove downtown on the day of the closing ceremonies and stood outside the stadium to watch.

It was incredible. Thousands of people from all over the world were there, along with reporters, television crews, and vendors of every kind. The police were on horseback, a sight you don't often see in Los Angeles. It was a day I'll never forget, though it wasn't the same as actually having assigned seats and fully participating. We were on the outside looking in, and that's never as much fun.

Are you on the outside looking in when it comes to your own life? Are you off to the side behind the barriers getting glimpses of the happenings but not fully participating? Are you enjoying the blessings that God has given you, or are you busy watching the progress or achievements of others and feeling inadequate?

Each one of us has an assigned seat in life. It's up to us to participate, make good decisions, run the race to the best of our ability, and celebrate when we make it over the finish line. In other words, it's up to us to go for the gold.

## THOUGHTS TO PONDER

Why do you think it's important for us to be actively involved in how our life turns out?

Do you feel you're missing out on your own life?

## BUMPER STICKER FOR THE DAY

You have only one life to live.
Be there for it.

## SCRIPTURE TO STAND ON

A righteous [man] can sing and be glad.

PROVERBS 29:6

## HELLO AGAIN, LORD...

Lord, don't let me get to the end of my life and not be able to answer what I did with it.

## SIXTY-FOUR

# A Life of Strife

Do you know people who love to stir up strife? The minute they hear someone say something negative about you, they rush to tell you all about it, right down to the very last detail. Never mind that it's going to hurt you. They figure you have a right to know.

True, they could have defended you to the person and peacefully taken care of the whole matter right then and there, without ever involving you. But what fun would that have been? It's a lot more entertaining to watch your face drop when they give you the whole, hurtful report.

Don't you wonder what drives someone like this? Chances are it's not friendship. It's the same thing that makes people want to take pictures of train wrecks. They thrive on having a ringside seat to a good wreck, no matter how many people have been hurt in the process.

Life's too short to waste your time with "friends" who instigate conflict, instead of looking for ways to resolve it. If you have some friends like this, pray for God to either change them or send you better friends—ones who'll be a friend first, and a reporter second.

## THOUGHTS TO PONDER

What do you think you should do the next time a "friend" relays a hurtful comment to you?

Why do you think some people like passing along hurtful reports to others?

## BUMPER STICKER FOR THE DAY

The measure of true friends isn't what they tell you that others say about you, but what they say about you to others.

## SCRIPTURE TO STAND ON

A greedy man stirs up dissension.

PROVERBS 28:25

## HELLO AGAIN, LORD...

Lord, thank you for giving us your example of friendship.

# SIXTY-FIVE

# Changing Lanes

The other day I was in a traffic jam. Well, the lane I was in was jammed. Hundreds, perhaps even thousands, of cars in front of me and behind me had come to a complete standstill. People were having tailgate parties and starting to exchange addresses for reunions.

My first thought was to change lanes. After all, the people in the lane next to me were zooming along, making great time and enjoying the journey. But I figured since no one else was moving over, they must know something I didn't. Clearly, the majority of the cars on the highway that day were in my lane. They couldn't all be wrong, could they?

So, there I sat, along with everyone else, not going anywhere and not doing anything about it but complaining. The solution was right there in front of my eyes—change lanes—but because no one else was doing it, I refused to do it, too.

In life we tend to want to follow the crowd, too. Because there are more people following their own way than are following God's, and they're usually a lot more vocal, we think they must know something we don't. So, we get in line behind them and go nowhere fast.

How foolish of us.

I finally wised up that day, though, and came to the realization that the problem had to be with the lane I had chosen. The people in that lane weren't going anywhere, and the longer I stayed behind them, the longer I wouldn't be going anywhere either. So I switched lanes and was eventually able to make it to my destination, safely and on time.

If you seem to have come to a dead standstill in your life,

maybe the problem isn't you. Maybe it's just the lane you've gotten yourself stuck in, maybe it's the crowd you've chosen to follow.

Maybe it's time you made a switch, too.

## THOUGHTS TO PONDER

Have you been following the crowd recently?

Why do you think the crowd doesn't always know the best way to go?

## BUMPER STICKER FOR THE DAY

> Before you follow someone, make sure
> that person is heading where you want to go.

## SCRIPTURE TO STAND ON

I walk in the way of righteousness,
along the paths of justice.

PROVERBS 8:20

## HELLO AGAIN, LORD...

Lord, help me to realize the majority is only right when they're following you.

# SIXTY-SIX

# A Tongue Sandwich

**D**id you ever have to bite your tongue? I'm not talking about chomping into your hamburger and getting a corner of your tongue instead. That hurts. What I'm talking about is when you bite your tongue so you'll keep quiet when what you'd really like to do is give someone a piece of your mind.

It's hard to keep silent when someone is treating you unfairly, teasing you, or challenging you to a duel of wits or fists. It's hard to take the peaceful route and walk away when the other route seems so much more satisfying. But that's what God, by Christ's example, tells us to do in most circumstances. Jesus never spoke up when it would have been contrary to the will of God to do so.

There were times, however, when Jesus did speak up, when he didn't bite his tongue. He spoke out when he was defending the weak, when it came to addressing self-righteous people, and when it came to proclaiming his message of hope.

So, if you're having a difficult time trying to figure out when to bite your tongue and when to go ahead and speak what's on your heart, ask yourself how Jesus would respond to your situation. If it would be contrary to the will of God to speak up, then bite your tongue. But if Christ would have boldly addressed the issue, then follow his example by doing it peacefully and in a spirit of love.

## THOUGHTS TO PONDER

Name some ways that a situation could get worse after we've spoken our mind.

What type of situation could get worse if we don't speak up?

## BUMPER STICKER FOR THE DAY

> Silence may be golden,
> but it's not always easy.

## SCRIPTURE TO STAND ON

Better a patient man than a warrior,
a man who controls his temper than one who takes a city.

PROVERBS 16:32

## HELLO AGAIN, LORD...

Lord, help me to keep quiet when you would have kept quiet, and to speak up when you would have spoken up.

# SIXTY-SEVEN

# Practice, Practice, Practice

I used to dream of becoming an Olympic ice skater. My first step toward realizing that dream was to spend some time on the ice. I figured an Olympic skater should probably do that. So I signed up for some lessons through my high school. We met at a local ice skating rink, and after only one lesson, I was doing figure eights, figure threes, and a variety of spins. Unfortunately, I was doing most of them on my backside.

By my next lesson, I had improved slightly. I was able to stay up on my feet all the way around the rink. I was able to do that by hanging on to the railing, of course, but at least I was vertical.

A few weeks later, I was confident enough to let go of the railing and replace it with the shirt of the guy skating in front of me. He didn't seem to mind. He kept yelling, "Hey, lady, get a grip!" but I'm sure that was his way of encouraging me to keep it up.

I did keep it up. I kept practicing and practicing. I showed up for class each week and never once lost sight of my dream. Eventually, I did become a pretty fair skater. I didn't make it to the Olympics, but I didn't make it to the emergency room, either.

Just as all that practice helped me improve my ice skating skills, practice helps us improve our faith walk, too. When we first start out with the Lord, most of us spend a good deal of time falling down. But the more we practice it, the better we get at it. Before long, we're able to let go of the railing, then the shirt of that person in front of us, until one day we realize we're not only making it around the rink all by ourselves, but we're doing figure eights and threes, and making our Teacher very proud.

## THOUGHTS TO PONDER

Have you been putting the necessary time in to improve your faith walk?

Why do you think God wants us to practice our faith daily?

## BUMPER STICKER FOR THE DAY

Spiritual muscles need exercise too.

## SCRIPTURE TO STAND ON

My son, give me your heart,
and let your eyes keep to my ways.

PROVERBS 23:26

## HELLO AGAIN, LORD...

Lord, help me to be as concerned about my progress as you are.

# SIXTY-EIGHT

# Department of Admissions

It's hard to admit when we're wrong, when we've messed up, botched it, failed miserably, goofed royally, and totally blown it. Our pride gets in the way and we sometimes end up defending our actions instead of admitting our blunder.

Rather than confess to our teacher that we didn't properly prepare for that oral report in history class, we decide to just get up there and wing it. We end up telling our classmates all about George Washington, the eighth President of the United States who was assassinated at Ford's Theater, leaving Vice President Theodore Roosevelt in charge of the sixty states of our union. (If you don't see the humor in the above, you need to start listening better in History!)

Rather than admit we shouldn't have ordered that third banana split, we simply sink our faces into it until our noses get freezer burn and our cholesterol level doubles.

For some reason, we'd rather look incompetent and be miserable, pout, hold grudges, wallow in self-pity, and be defensive than admit we've made a mistake. We'll defend our mistake, risking our health and well-being, all because we can't verbalize three little words, "I blew it." Umm ... that wasn't so hard to say after all.

## THOUGHTS TO PONDER

Why do you think it's so difficult to admit when we're wrong?

What good things might come from being able to admit we're wrong?

## BUMPER STICKER FOR THE DAY

No one is always wrong.
But everyone has been at least once.

## SCRIPTURE TO STAND ON

Like an earring of gold or an ornament of fine gold
is a wise man's rebuke to a listening ear.

PROVERBS 25:12

## HELLO AGAIN, LORD...

Lord, give me the courage to admit when I'm wrong, so we can
fix it together.

# SIXTY-NINE

# Between You, Me, the Gatepost ... and Four Hundred Other People

ossip. It comes in a variety of imaginative disguises. We call it "confiding," "getting advice," "sharing," and a host of other benign terms. But whatever title we use to gloss over it, we're not fooling God.

Check out Romans 1:29-30. God warns against "being filled with all unrighteousness, fornication, wickedness, covetousness, maliciousness, envy, murder, debate, deceit, malignity, whisperers, backbiters, haters of God, spiteful, proud, boasters...."

Now, why would God list whisperers and backbiters along with murderers, fornicators, and haters of God? I'd say it's because he doesn't like any of those behaviors very much.

Not stopping gossip when we hear it is wrong, too. We try to excuse ourselves by saying that we're only listening to the gossip. We didn't start it. But when a dam breaks and water is flooding the streets, the emergency workers don't get to the scene and say, "Hey, we didn't break the dam, so it's not our responsibility to do anything about it." If they did, the floodwaters would keep coming until everyone drowned.

Gossip is like floodwaters. We may not have set the flood in motion, but we can do our part to help stop it. God gave us our mouths for blessing, not destruction. Instead of standing by and watching the water flow past us, maybe it's time we rebuilt the dam.

## THOUGHTS TO PONDER

Have you recently passed along a story without checking out the facts with the people involved?

If someone heard a false rumor about you, how would you want them to handle it?

## BUMPER STICKER FOR THE DAY

> Dirt shouldn't be the diet of Christians.

## SCRIPTURE TO STAND ON

With his mouth the godless destroys his neighbor.

PROVERBS 11:9

## HELLO AGAIN, LORD...

Lord, help me to be a gossip stopper and not a gossip starter.

# SEVENTY

# He Likes Us

One of the Academy Awards' most memorable clips was when Sally Field won an Oscar for Best Actress of 1984 for her role in Tri-Star's *Places in the Heart*. She closed her acceptance speech with, "I can't deny the fact that you like me—right now, you *like* me!" It was an emotional moment. Sally had come to realize that not only did her peers respect her as an actress and admire her determination and career choices, but they *liked* her, too.

Do you know that God *likes* us? Sure, he loves us, but he *likes* us, too. He enjoys spending time with us. He misses us when we're too busy for him. It hurts him to be left out of our plans, our problems, our lives.

When Adam and Eve hid in the Garden of Eden after eating of the forbidden fruit, God didn't call out Adam's name, then say, "Aha! I caught you! You did the very thing I told you not to do! I can't turn my back for a second! Well, you blew it, kids! This time you really blew it!"

He did call out Adam's name, but it was more of a beckoning by a father who knew something was wrong with his children. God enjoyed spending time with his creation and was heartbroken that they were now hiding from him in shame. Sure, he was disappointed in their disobedience, but he was more disappointed in the fact that their relationship had changed.

God wants an ongoing relationship with us. Why? Because he *loves* us. And he *likes* us. It hurts him when we willingly disobey and make choices that damage that relationship.

## THOUGHTS TO PONDER

Has something come between you and God?

How do you feel about the fact that God *likes* you and wants to spend time with you?

## BUMPER STICKER FOR THE DAY

> **When God calls,
> he doesn't like to be put on hold.**

## SCRIPTURE TO STAND ON

Goodwill is found among the upright.

PROVERBS 14:9

## HELLO AGAIN, LORD...

Lord, help me not to be selfish with the attention I give you.

# SEVENTY-ONE
## Even Steven

When we've been hurt by someone, our natural instinct is to get even. If they say a cutting remark to us, we want to say one right back to them. If they abandon us when we need them, we want to take our phone off the hook so they can't reach us the next time they're hurting. We want to keep the score even. We're not happy until those who have hurt us are unhappy, too.

The funny thing about getting even, though, is that it never feels as good as we imagine it will. We might accomplish what we set out to do, giving them a taste of their own medicine, but that medicine doesn't taste very good to us, either.

The Bible tells us that the best way to get even with someone is to leave the matter in God's hands, not praying for their destruction, but praying for God's will in their lives. God promised to even up the score, and he can do it in ways we can't even imagine.

Moses didn't have to get even with Pharaoh. God did it for him. He opened up the Red Sea for Moses and all the Israelites, then closed it just as Pharaoh's men tried to cross. I doubt if a plan like that ever crossed Moses' mind. He probably was praying something like "Lord, make all of Pharaoh's chariots have flat tires," or "Give that ol' Pharaoh the worst hair day of his life!"

But God did Moses one better. He miraculously split the Red Sea and gave Moses a payback to Pharaoh that had to have made the front page of every newspaper in Egypt!

So, if it seems like your enemies are scoring more often than you, if they appear to be gaining on you, don't worry. Leave the matter in God's hands, and trust him to even up the score. He's got a lot more creativity than we'll ever have, and who knows, he might even perform the greatest miracle of all—transforming that person into a friend.

## THOUGHTS TO PONDER
Have you ever wanted to pay someone back for a wrong they did to you?

Why do you think God wants us to leave revenge in his hands?

## BUMPER STICKER FOR THE DAY

> If you're always looking to get even, you'll never be in balance.

## SCRIPTURE TO STAND ON
Do not say, "I'll do for him as he has done to me."

PROVERBS 24:29

## HELLO AGAIN, LORD...
Lord, help me to trust your ways, your plans, and your defense strategy.

# SEVENTY-TWO

# Heavy Meddlers

No, this chapter isn't about the musical kind of heavy metalers. It's about heavy *meddlers*—people who thrive on interfering in others' affairs. Perhaps you've ran into a few of them. They're eager to tell you exactly what to do, how to do it, and when to do it, but their opinion is the only thing they offer. They don't offer help, encouragement, or any of those things that you could really use.

I've often wondered what drives someone to meddle. Maybe they're just bored. Or maybe they're really trying to help, but they just don't know how. Or it could be that they're just nosy. Who knows?

The bottom line is this: if the meddler is offering good advice, by all means take it. Good advice is good advice, no matter who it's coming from or how it's presented. But if what they're saying is bad counsel or only intended to discourage you, then don't think twice about it. Don't allow meddlesome comments to defeat you or cause you to lose faith in the good that God is wanting for your life.

## THOUGHTS TO PONDER

What do you think makes someone want to meddle in the affairs of another person?

How can you tell whether someone is wanting to help you or merely wanting to meddle?

## BUMPER STICKER FOR THE DAY

> The best way to judge the value
> of someone's advice? Count the times
> they've taken it themselves.

## SCRIPTURE TO STAND ON

It is to a man's honor to avoid strife,
but every fool is quick to quarrel.

PROVERBS 20:3

## HELLO AGAIN, LORD...

Lord, remind me that the difference between meddling and helping is one I do for my benefit and the other I do for someone else's.

# SEVENTY-THREE

# Weak Spots

**M**any of us have been taught all our lives to be brave, to stand tall in the face of adversity, to not let "the other side" know when they've gotten to us. That may be good advice for athletes, but there are times in life when we really do need to let our vulnerabilities show.

What good does it do to pretend we can handle it all when we're falling apart? Who can help us if we're putting up a facade of strength, or pretending that we've got everything under control?

God didn't say, "Get to the end of your rope first, then I'll help you." He said he'd help us whenever and wherever we call on him. But too often we wait until the rope has already started unraveling before admitting we've got a problem. It doesn't have to be that way. We can call on God whether we're at the end of our rope, the middle, or at the very beginning.

Until we give up and give the matter over to God, admitting our vulnerability, acknowledging we're weak and need his arms to lean on, our problems will stay in our hands. Our only choice then will be to handle them with our own resources, our own wisdom, and our own strength. Is that what we really want?

## THOUGHTS TO PONDER

Have you been pretending that you can handle a problem alone?

What do you think is keeping you from handing it over to the Lord?

## BUMPER STICKER FOR THE DAY

> You don't have to know all the answers
> as long as you're teamed up
> with the One who does.

## SCRIPTURE TO STAND ON

Through me your days will be many,
and years will be added to your life.

PROVERBS 9:11

## HELLO AGAIN, LORD...

Even though you're a God of miracles, help me not to wait until the last second to call on you in my hour of need.

# SEVENTY-FOUR

# Right On!

**N**one of us like to have our rights infringed upon. When someone goes through our personal belongings, cuts in line in front of us, wears our clothing without asking, reads our diary, eavesdrops on our conversations, or tells us to clear the telephone line right in the middle of our two-hour summation of last night's sleepover, we get upset and immediately let them know they've violated our rights. Our rights are precious to us and we want to protect them.

Other people have rights, too, though, and we don't always see that. We don't realize that by demanding our rights, we might be infringing on someone else's.

We may have the right to play our music as loudly as we want to, but if it's so loud our neighbors can't hear that volcano erupting behind them, then it's infringing on their right to seek safety in a timely manner.

We might have the right to refuse to bathe for a week, but our family also has the right not to have to bear the expense of hiring a live-in exterminator.

Unless we're residing on a deserted island, we can't live however we want to live. We have to consider other people's rights, not just our own, and often that means we have to compromise.

What do I mean by compromise? We have the right to free speech, but if we're exercising it while our classmates are trying to hear the teacher, then they're being denied their right to learn. At that moment, we need to forego our right to speech. That way we, along with our classmates, can exercise our right to learn.

We have the right to make our own decisions, but our parents have the right to make rules, rules which our rights can't supersede. Of course, if the rules are abusive—if your right to health and safety are being violated—then you'll need to tell a trusted friend, family member, pastor, or someone else who can help.

If you simply don't like the rules, though, then you need to realize that your parents have the right to protect you and raise you the best way they know how. That might mean they deny you your right to go camping in a blizzard or go to that unsupervised party this Friday night, but that's their right.

Rights—to properly exercise yours, you need to let others exercise theirs, too.

## THOUGHTS TO PONDER

Have you ever thought your rights were infringed upon? How did it make you feel?

Do you think you've ever infringed upon the rights of others? If so, what do you think you should have done differently?

## BUMPER STICKER FOR THE DAY

It's not always right to demand our rights.

## SCRIPTURE TO STAND ON

A man's pride shall bring him low,
but a man of lowly spirit gains honor.

PROVERBS 29:23

## HELLO AGAIN, LORD...

Lord, help me to remember that you had the right and the power to stop your crucifixion, but for our sake you didn't.

# SEVENTY-FIVE

# The End of the World?

**M**y oldest sister, Linda, had diabetes from the time she was four years old. Over the years, I witnessed some pretty frightening episodes because of it—comas, convulsions, infections that wouldn't heal—you name it, she had it. Needless to say, when I was diagnosed with diabetes at eighteen years of age, I thought it was the end of my world.

I remember going to my church that very next Sunday and asking the visiting minister, who happened to be a medical doctor, to pray for me. He did, then sensing my fear, he added the words, "Don't worry. You're going to be all right."

Over the years, I've held onto the prayer and those words, and looking back today, I can happily say he was right. Not that diabetes hasn't affected my life. It has. I've had to take insulin injections, every day for over two decades. I prick my finger several times a day to test my blood sugar level. I've had to watch what I eat, keep candy in my purse at all times in case my blood sugar level drops unexpectedly, carefully monitor any cuts and infections, and maintain a regular exercise program.

Yes, diabetes has changed my world, but it wasn't the end of it. I've never gone into a coma, had a convulsion, or had an infection that wouldn't heal. In fact, since developing diabetes, I eat healthier and am probably in better physical condition than I was before.

Throughout your life you might have to face situations which on the surface look like the end of your world. But don't give in to that fear. Fear has a way of magnifying the severity of our crisis and leaving us emotionally paralyzed. In other words, that which we think is the end of our world might just turn out to be a new beginning.

## THOUGHTS TO PONDER

Have you ever had to face something that you thought was the "end of your world"? Write it down..

What positive things do you think might come from this crisis?

## BUMPER STICKER FOR THE DAY

> The Red Sea looked like an obstacle, but God made it a path of deliverance.

## SCRIPTURE TO STAND ON

Blessed is he who trusts in the Lord.

PROVERBS 16:20

## HELLO AGAIN, LORD...

Lord, may I have courage to face the challenges that come my way and unwavering trust in your love.

# SEVENTY-SIX

# Choices

Throughout our lives we're faced with all kinds of choices. Baskin and Robbins gives us thirty-one of them. We can choose regular unleaded or supreme unleaded; first class or coach; French, Italian, Ranch, or Thousand Island dressing. Sometimes we're going to feel like a nut and want an Almond Joy. Other times we're going to crave a Mounds. The choice is ours.

When we make those kinds of choices, there aren't a lot of consequences. We may get better gas mileage with the regular unleaded than we do the supreme, and we'll have more leg room and a much thinner wallet if we fly first class instead of coach, but these aren't life-changing decisions.

Other choices, though, have more serious consequences. Choices about sex, drugs, smoking, running away, the kinds of friends we hang with, obeying laws, and so on are choices we're faced with, too. It's up to us to make the right choices in those instances.

Our parents may have rules that can guide us into making good choices, but if we're only doing those right things to please them, and not from our own convictions, when we're old enough to decide for ourselves, we'll make wrong choices.

So, remember—the next time you have a serious decision to make, make the right one, but make it for you. Then, when you look back on your life someday, you'll be able to say "I, more than anyone else, treated myself with respect."

## THOUGHTS TO PONDER

Why do you think we're ultimately responsible for the choices we make?

Which do you honestly feel you're more concerned with—respecting yourself or pleasing your friends?

## BUMPER STICKER FOR THE DAY

> **When you just say no,
> you say yes to so much more.**

## SCRIPTURE TO STAND ON

Do not swerve to the right or to the left;
keep your foot from evil.

PROVERBS 4:27

## HELLO AGAIN, LORD...

Lord, help me to realize the importance of making the right decisions.

SEVENTY-SEVEN

# Where Always Is Heard
## a Discouraging Word

On the range there may never be heard a discouraging word, but it's not always that way in our schools, jobs, and sometimes even in our families. Not everyone is an encourager. Some people have the gift, if you can call it that, of *dis*couragement.

No matter how hard you try to get good grades, practice the piano, improve your appearance, attitude, or life choices, these discouragers refuse to say anything positive. Bring home a report card with five A's and a B, and a discourager will look right past the A's verbally chastise you for the B. Sit at that piano until your legs go numb, and all someone like this can say is "You'll never be as good as so and so." Get your hair cut and they'll point out the four hairs the stylist missed without saying a word about how cute the new look is on you.

When dealing with discouragers, you should realize the problem usually lies within themselves. It has little or nothing to do with you. It could be that the discourager never heard an encouraging word as a child, and so a negative response to a positive effort is all they know how to give. Or maybe they have such low self-esteem that discouraging others is their way of building their self-image. Or maybe they just want to be mean.

Whatever the reason, don't let their cutting remarks or even their silence become your assessment of yourself. If you truly are doing your best, God sees that. He knows how hard you're trying, and he wants to encourage you. He wants you to know how valuable you are to him. He wants you to have as much faith in yourself as he has in you. The Bible is full of positive reinforcements. If you're not getting the encouragement you need from the people in your life, get it from him. He has an endless supply.

## THOUGHTS TO PONDER

Do you feel like you could use an encouraging word right now?

What proof do we have that God believes in us?

## BUMPER STICKER FOR THE DAY

Believe in yourself.
God does.

## SCRIPTURE TO STAND ON

[God] delights in those whose ways are blameless.

PROVERBS 11:20

## HELLO AGAIN, LORD...

Thank you, Lord, for believing in me, even when I may not believe in myself.

# SEVENTY-EIGHT

## Promises, Promises

Your best friend borrows ten bucks, and promises to pay it right back. If you're counting on that money to buy your ticket to the football game Friday night, you'll be pretty disappointed if she lets you down, won't you?

If your dad promises to take you fishing on Saturday, but a meeting comes up at work and he chooses to go there instead, you'll feel he let you down, right?

Sure, you will. It's aggravating when someone gives you his or her word, then breaks it. It hurts and disappoints you.

Others don't like it when we disappoint them, either.

Do you realize when you tell your teacher you're going to improve your grades, and don't, you're breaking your word? When you tell your parents you're going to quit teasing your little brother or sister, and you don't follow through on your promise, do you know you're letting them down, too?

We need to be as determined to keep our word as we want others to be with their word to us. God sets the perfect example for this. He always keeps his word. He said we could trust him, that he'd never leave us or forsake us, and to this day he's kept his word. When God makes a promise, he follows through on it.

We should follow through on the promises we make, too.

## THOUGHTS TO PONDER

When you make a promise, do you do your best to keep your word?

Why do you think it's important to follow through on your promises?

## BUMPER STICKER FOR THE DAY

In a world where so much is disposable, there's one thing we should always keep— our word.

## SCRIPTURE TO STAND ON

A faithful man will be richly blessed.

PROVERBS 28:20

## HELLO AGAIN, LORD...

Lord, help me to keep the promises I make, especially the ones I make to you.

# SEVENTY-NINE
## Repair Shop

**H**ave you ever tried to fix something, only to make matters worse? Last night my husband announced that he was going to fix the plumbing in our bathroom. Whenever we flushed the toilet, it would continue to make a whooshing sound for five or ten minutes. I didn't really mind it because if I closed my eyes, I could pretend we were vacationing at Niagara Falls or some exotic place; but the constant noise was getting on his nerves.

Being the handyman that he is, he got in the car, drove to the plumbing store, bought all the right supplies, and worked on the toilet into the night. Now, instead of Niagara Falls, we have a geyser! Sure, it's giving us some extra money from the tourists, but our toilet still isn't working properly. We're going to have to call a professional plumber to fix the original problem and reverse any damage we may have done.

Sometimes when we get involved in situations and try to fix them, it only makes matters worse. No matter how well intentioned we are, our actions can backfire on us. That advice we eagerly give our best friend, and that he or she so trustingly follows, might not turn out the way we think it will. It could produce a bigger mess than before. That argument between our parents, the one we get in the middle of and try to defuse, might intensify instead.

So then, if there are no guarantees how a situation is going to turn out, if we run the risk of something exploding in our faces, why would we ever want to get involved in the first place? Because we don't know what the outcome will be until we try. My husband has fixed many things around our house and has saved us a lot of money doing that. Plumbing just doesn't happen to be one of the things he's good at. But he didn't know that until he tried.

Whatever situations are in your life right now, there will be some which you'll discover you can indeed fix. There'll be others that are serious enough to seek professional advice. And then there'll be a few that are so broken that only God can repair the damage. In those situations, it's good to remember that the Good Samaritan helped the wounded man most by taking him to someone who could heal his wounds. Often, taking our loved ones to Someone who can heal their wounds is the best thing we can do, too.

## THOUGHTS TO PONDER
Is there a situation that you've been trying to intervene in, but don't seem to be getting anywhere?

Why do you think it's important that we leave the end result up to God?

## BUMPER STICKER FOR THE DAY

> **Some situations are beyond our capabilities to fix. No situation is beyond his.**

## SCRIPTURE TO STAND ON
A man's spirit sustains him in sickness,
but a crushed spirit who can bear?

PROVERBS 18:14

## HELLO AGAIN, LORD...
Help me, Lord, to get involved when I should, keep quiet when I need to, and always leave the outcome to you.

# EIGHTY

# Chain Link Prayer

This morning I received an e-mail from Mark Lowry. He had an urgent family need—his three-year-old nephew had wandered off from his home and had been missing all night. Mark was asking everyone on his e-mail list, all thirty thousand of them, to unite in prayer over the situation. Nothing like having an army on your side!

I just received Mark's second e-mail. The boy was found this afternoon, sitting by a lake. Prayer works.

E-mailed prayer requests are the newest way to get the word out of someone's need. The telephone prayer chain is another way. With a telephone prayer chain, the first person on the list calls the next person on the list, who calls the next person, and so on until everyone has been notified.

What's great about prayer chains and Internet prayer requests is how quickly the word can get out. Within seconds, people can be joining with you in prayer. Then, those people might call three of their friends to pray, who call three of their friends to pray, and ... well, you get the picture.

When we have needs, it's comforting to know that people everywhere are praying. And the more Christians you have praying with you, the more there'll be to rejoice with you when the answer comes.

## THOUGHTS TO PONDER

Are you a member of a prayer chain? If not, what's keeping you from starting one?

Why do you think prayer works?

## BUMPER STICKER FOR THE DAY

> Prayer chains are one of the few chains
> God doesn't want broken.

## SCRIPTURE TO STAND ON

The Lord detests the sacrifice of the wicked,
but the prayer of the upright pleases him.

PROVERBS 15:8

## HELLO AGAIN, LORD...

Lord, thank you for those who have ever uttered my name or my need in their prayers.

# EIGHTY-ONE

# Circles

The next time you get the chance, watch a hamster working out on his exercise wheel. You'll see him huffing and puffing, little sweatband on his head, drinking Gatorade from his water tube. He'll be looking good. He'll be looking healthy. He'll be having the time of his life—so much so that you won't have the heart to tell him all he's doing is going in circles. Hour after hour, day after day, 'round and 'round he goes. Exciting? To him it is. Why? Because he chooses to make it exciting. He doesn't greet each morning by grumbling, "Oh, whoopee, I get to ride the exercise wheel again." No. He doesn't sit in the corner feeling sorry for himself, moping because there's nothing to do. He makes the best of his situation and hops on that wheel and gives it everything he's got.

Do you greet your day with that same kind of enthusiasm or do you sit in the corner of your bedroom grumbling that there's nothing to do and nowhere to go? So what if it's the same-o, same-o. Do it with such enthusiasm that it'll feel like a brand new activity every time you do it.

But don't stop there. If there truly isn't anything to do in your town, why not plan something? Be creative. Get a group of your friends together and come up with an idea for a community event, or something special for just the teens in your area. Talk to your parents, your teachers, civic leaders, and whoever else you can think of to help. Solicit financial support from local businesses.

Like the hamster, fun isn't something that's always going to come to you. Sometimes you have to make it yourself.

## THOUGHTS TO PONDER

What do you do when you're bored?

What's stopping you from planning a fun event with your school, your family, or your community?

## BUMPER STICKER FOR THE DAY

It takes U to have F-U-N.

## SCRIPTURE TO STAND ON

The light of the righteous shines brightly.

PROVERBS 13:9

## HELLO AGAIN, LORD...

Lord, help me not only to bloom where I'm planted, but to dance in the breezes while I'm doing it!

# EIGHTY-TWO

# One Is the Loneliest Number

The barber looked up and nodded as the old man entered the shop and took a seat. My husband and three young sons were in line for a haircut, along with several other people. The old man was going to have quite a wait. Everyone in town, it seemed, had waited until after Christmas to get their hair cut.

It was December 26, and each of our boys had a lap full of new toys to help pass the time. It turned out to be an unnecessary precaution because the barber was fast. He had the other customers and our sons done so quickly I hardly got to finish the magazine article I had settled down to read.

As my husband went to the counter to pay the bill, I couldn't help but overhear the barber talking to the old man.

"So, what did Santa Claus bring you?" he asked, motioning for the old man to sit in the barber chair.

"Oh," the old man said, "Santa didn't come to my house this year."

"Weren't you a good boy?" the barber teased.

"No one's come to see me for years," the old man said. "Why would Santa?"

The barber didn't say any more. He just cut his hair. But I watched as tears began to well up in the old man's eyes.

Most people don't choose to be alone. Often it's a result of circumstances beyond their control—their spouse passes away, they lose contact with or outlive their children, or maybe they've never had any children. For whatever reason, many people find themselves facing their later years alone with no one to visit, call, or even think twice about them.

God loves them, he hasn't forgotten about them, but how will they ever know it unless they see his love in us?

## THOUGHTS TO PONDER

Is there someone who could use a visit or a phone call from you today?

Why do you think we shouldn't forsake the elderly?

## BUMPER STICKER FOR THE DAY

> **Could you be the answer to someone's prayers?**

## SCRIPTURE TO STAND ON

Gray hair is a crown of splendor;
it is attained by a righteous life.

PROVERBS 16:31

## HELLO AGAIN, LORD...

Lord, show me someone who needs an encouraging word from you today.

# EIGHTY-THREE

# Watch Your Step

**W**hen I was a teenager, I spent a week at summer camp. I went swimming, horseback riding, ice skating, and hiking, and met a cabin full of new friends. The cafeteria food left something to be desired, though (roadkill and tater tots just aren't my thing). My favorite activity was sitting around the campfire every night singing camp songs (that's probably why the bears stayed away).

On the final day, a group of us decided to get in one last hike before heading back home. Grabbing our jackets, a canteen of water, and a few snacks, we headed off into the wilderness. After walking for about an hour along scenic trails, through cool mountain streams, and over rocky terrain, it became clear to us that we were in the very presence of God. We were surrounded by his creative handiwork. We were also extremely lost!

Being the brave campers that we were, we immediately started yelling "Help!" as loudly as we could. We wrote S.O.S. with some nearby rocks. We were so convinced that we were going to die, we began sharing our last wills and testaments with each other. One boy left his school jacket to his girlfriend, a girl left her stamp collection to her baby brother, and I was just about to leave my recipe book to science, when someone heard the sound of a car driving by.

"Shh! Listen!" she said.

We listened and heard another car drive by. Then another. And another. Wait a minute! We weren't lost! We were just off the highway. All we had to do was climb up the hillside about twenty feet and we were back to civilization.

So one by one we climbed. I was the last one to reach the road, and I'll never forget the words of one of my fellow campers when

I took that final step. "Now that you're up here," he said, "I'll tell you."

"Tell me what?" I asked, panting.

"See that rock over there, that last one you stepped on?"

I glanced down at the rock. "Yeah. What about it?"

"See that stick underneath it?"

"That big one in the shade?"

He nodded. "It's a snake."

We were about two miles away from camp. I think I made it back in four minutes flat!

I learned a good lesson that day. By not watching my step, I placed myself in danger and didn't even realize it.

We should always pay attention to the steps we take in life, too.

## THOUGHTS TO PONDER

Have you made any missteps lately?

Could they have placed you in a dangerous situation that you aren't even aware of?

## BUMPER STICKER FOR THE DAY

> A minor misstep can have major consequences.

## SCRIPTURE TO STAND ON

Make level paths for your feet
and take only ways that are firm.

PROVERBS 4:26

## HELLO AGAIN, LORD...

Lord, help me to watch my step every step of the way.

# EIGHTY-FOUR

# Turtles on the Half Shell

**H**ave you ever seen a turtle on its back? It looks pretty ridiculous struggling to turn itself over, doesn't it? I wonder if that's how we look to God when we struggle to turn our lives around all by ourselves.

Some of us seem to think that, before we can come to the Lord, we have to impress him by how much we can take care of on our own. We say we'll give our lives to God as soon as we stop this bad habit or clean up this mess that we've gotten ourselves into.

But God doesn't love us because of how much we can do on our own or how little we need him. He loves us because we need him every minute of every day. He knows that without him we're like turtles on our back, frantically waving out feet, not really getting anywhere. He continues to love us in our helpless state, totally dependent on him, willing to recognize and admit our need.

If we let him, he's the one who'll get us back on our feet again.

## THOUGHTS TO PONDER

Have you been trying to clean up a situation in your life on your own?

Why do you think God wants us to come to him with our needs?

## BUMPER STICKER FOR THE DAY

> Some people haven't been rescued
> because they've never yelled "Help!"

## SCRIPTURE TO STAND ON

He who conceals his sins does not prosper,
but whoever confesses and  renounces them finds mercy.

PROVERBS 28:13

## HELLO AGAIN, LORD...

I'm grateful, Lord, that I can come to you in my helplessness.

# EIGHTY-FIVE

# Passing Thoughts

I used to think about telling the clerk at the grocery store near my home how much I appreciated her happy disposition. But the last time I was in there they told me she had moved on to another job.

The thought crossed my mind several times to tell my mailman how much I looked forward to his smile and the friendly comments he'd share whenever I saw him, but he retired before I got around to it.

For weeks I thought about telling my pastor how much I love and appreciate him. Then one Sunday he announced that he was resigning.

Passing thoughts. How many times do people cross our minds, but we don't act on those feelings? We get so caught up in the whirlwind of our own problems and daily schedules that we never seem to get around to doing them. We just don't know the difficulties people around us are facing every day. They may not say anything or act like they need it, but they may be crying out inside for God to send an encouraging word their way.

One Sunday morning during a particularly tough time in my life, I was sitting in church praying for God to lead someone to say something encouraging to me. God didn't let me down. But those from whom I would have expected encouragement weren't the ones God used to give it. It was a gentle, quiet, unassuming lady in the church who came to me after the service and spoke the words I needed to hear. I'll never forget how God's love was demonstrated to me through that woman, and how thankful I was that she followed through on what God was leading her to do.

If you feel God leading you to say something encouraging to someone, do it. For that need at that moment, you just might be the only one listening to him.

## THOUGHTS TO PONDER
Do you have an encouraging word you're supposed to be sharing with someone today?

Why do you think God puts it on our hearts to encourage one another at just the right moment?

## BUMPER STICKER FOR THE DAY

Regrets make lousy souvenirs.

## SCRIPTURE TO STAND ON
A word aptly spoken is like apples of gold in settings of silver.
PROVERBS 25:11

## HELLO AGAIN, LORD...
Lord, help me to remember that encouragement has to be spoken for it to count.

# EIGHTY-SIX

## All Charges Dropped

Actor Peter Falk once said, "Being chased by Columbo is like being nibbled to death by a duck."

Guilt is a bit like that, too. We may try to forget about our wrongdoing, but it won't let us go. It just keeps nibbling away at us, day in and day out, until we can't take it anymore. That's when we need to take it to the cross.

None of us are perfect. Think of the most responsible people you know, the most reliable, the ones you'd never picture messing up. Guess what? They mess up, too. Everyone, whether you'll ever know about it or not, messes up from time to time. It's human nature.

So go easy on yourself. Walking with the Lord is like running in a race. If you fall on the track, you don't just lie there getting trampled by the rest of the runners. You get up, get back on your feet, and start running again.

## THOUGHTS TO PONDER

Is there some failure that you're not forgiving yourself for?

If you've asked God's forgiveness and believe you've been forgiven, why do you think you aren't forgiving yourself?

## BUMPER STICKER FOR THE DAY

> **How many races are won by imperfect people? All of them.**

## SCRIPTURE TO STAND ON

For though a righteous man falls seven times, he rises again.

PROVERBS 24:16

## HELLO AGAIN, LORD...

Lord, help me to be as quick to forgive myself as you are to forgive me.

# EIGHTY-SEVEN

# Blowin' in the Wind

Whenever a tornado warning has been issued, a ribbon of information crawls across the bottom of our television screen. Besides telling viewers to take cover, it also advises anyone who happens to be in a trailer at that moment to seek shelter in a more permanent structure.

Why? Because tornadoes have been known to juggle trailers in the air like a circus act. Most trailers don't have a permanent foundation like a house. When a storm hits, a mobile home can really become mobile!

Without a firm foundation, our faith can become mobile, too. It can be blown around in the winds of persecution, disaster, sickness, or whatever else comes our way. That's why we need to grow as close to God as we can during the good times. We need to build up a firm foundation by reading his Word, praying, and growing in his ways, so that when one of the storms of life hits, we won't be blown into Oz.

Once the storm passes and its destructive force is evident all around us, people will see then that we're unshaken, our faith is intact, and we haven't moved an inch except to draw closer to him.

## THOUGHTS TO PONDER

Do you feel you have a strong enough foundation for when the storms of life hit?

If not, what steps should you be taking now to build up your faith?

## BUMPER STICKER FOR THE DAY

> **How you survive a storm all depends on how well you've prepared for it.**

## SCRIPTURE TO STAND ON

He who trusts in the Lord will prosper.

PROVERBS 28:25

## HELLO AGAIN, LORD...

Lord, help my faith in you to be stronger than any storm that may come my way.

# EIGHTY-EIGHT
# Change of Address

The other day I bought a new address book. It was long over-due. My old one still had the phone number of the doctor who delivered me at birth.

I'm now in the process of transferring all the information from the old book into the new one. It's quite a job. There are addresses in there that have been crossed out and replaced with other addresses that have been crossed out and replaced with still other addresses. The people in my life do a lot of moving. (My cooking probably has a lot to do with that.)

An address book can reveal a lot about our lives. It can show us which numbers we call most often (those are the pages with the most doodling), and it shows the numbers we call least often (like Dial-a-Polka). It tells us how many friends we have whose last names begin with "M" and how few we have whose last names begin with "X."

Most of all, address books reveal our changing relationships. Some addresses are crossed out because our friends have moved away. One or two friends' names may be crossed out because they've passed away. There might be listings of friends who turned out to be less than friends, and listings of friends who turned out to be more like family. Some names we will have known since childhood, and others will be brand new acquain-tances.

Our address books tell us how many people have crossed our paths throughout our lifetime. For some of those people, we may be their only connection to Jesus.

## THOUGHTS TO PONDER

Would you say that most of the people listed in your address book are believers?

Of the ones who aren't, what do you think their chances are of hearing about Jesus from someone other than yourself?

## BUMPER STICKER FOR THE DAY

> It's called the "Good News,"
> not the "Good Secret."

## SCRIPTURE TO STAND ON

The fruit of the righteous is a tree of life;
and he who wins souls is wise.

PROVERBS 11:30

## HELLO AGAIN, LORD...

Lord, thank you for the people you've brought into my life, and for the reasons you might have for doing so.

# EIGHTY-NINE

# Piece by Piece

Do you feel as though your life is falling apart piece by piece? Have you been making one bad decision after another? Do you find yourself wondering how much more you can take, how much longer you can hold on?

Life can get tough. Our tomorrows don't always deliver what we hoped they would. We get disappointed and discouraged. But giving up isn't the answer. It takes courage to keep going in spite of our problems. It takes courage to wait and see what the next day might bring, and the next, and the next.

Courage is hard, though. It's easier to complain and think we're the only ones with problems. Why can't our family get along like other families? Why isn't that person having to struggle over the things I have to battle? Why doesn't anything bad ever happen to them?

The funny thing is, if we'd spend a little time talking to those whose lives seem so perfect, we'd no doubt discover that life hasn't been easy for them, either. We might even go away thanking God for our problems in light of the seriousness of theirs.

So, when circumstances start to overwhelm us, should we panic? Should we complain? No. We should just take each problem as it comes, knowing that God is there to help us with it. And above all else, we need to hang in there. Why? Because Jesus hung in there for us.

## THOUGHTS TO PONDER

Is there something that you've been discouraged about?

What proof do you have that God cares about your disappointments?

## BUMPER STICKER FOR THE DAY

> Can't seem to hold your life together?
> Try a few nails. His.

## SCRIPTURE TO STAND ON

For whoever finds me finds life.

PROVERBS 8:35

## HELLO AGAIN, LORD...

Lord, when I'm down, help me to look up.

# NINETY

# The Finish Line

Are you a procrastinator? Do you put things off until the last possible moment? Have you been known to stay up half the night cramming for an exam that you've known about for three weeks? Do you put off cleaning your room until you can't find your way out?

Whenever I've been tempted to procrastinate, I tell myself that the project, job, chore, or whatever isn't going to go away until I finish it. It'll keep hanging over my head, half-done, not doing anybody any good—least of all me. Half of a bridge isn't a bridge. It's a mandatory car wash. It can't take anyone anywhere except into the water.

There's no sense of accomplishment in unfinished projects. You can't list them on your resumé: "Wrote first ten pages of a television script. Plan to get back to it someday."

"Started work on designing a new computer program. Got sidetracked with other endeavors, but will be completing it soon."

"Volunteered to drive hot meals to the elderly. That was two weeks ago.... Hope they've got a microwave."

Have you ever thought about where we'd be if Jesus hadn't finished the work he was given to do? What if he had only made it to the edge of Golgatha and turned back? Would that have done any of us any good?

Of course not. The work had to be completed to count. Our work, if we want it to count, has to be completed, too. The world is full of people who make promises and are full of good intentions. What separates them from the winners is often only one step, one step over the finish line.

## THOUGHTS TO PONDER

Do you have something that you've been procrastinating about?

What do you think is keeping you from finishing it?

## BUMPER STICKER FOR THE DAY

> **When we see Jesus, we want him to say "Well done," not "Well started."**

## SCRIPTURE TO STAND ON

The path of the righteous is like the first gleam of dawn, shining ever brighter till the full light of day.

PROVERBS 4:18

## HELLO AGAIN, LORD ...

Lord, thank you for your promise of completing the good work you've begun in me.

# Answers to devotion thirty-three

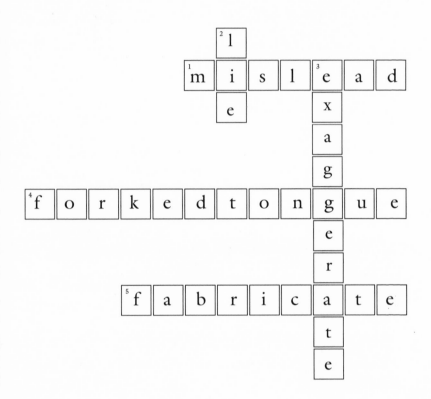